I0449214

ADP 1
THE ARMY

SEPTEMBER 2012

DISTRIBUTION RESTRICTION:
Approved for public release; distribution is unlimited.

HEADQUARTERS, DEPARTMENT OF THE ARMY

The Soldier's Creed and Warrior Ethos

I am an American Soldier.

I am a warrior and a member of a team.

I serve the people of the United States,
and live the Army Values.

I will always place the mission first.

I will never accept defeat.

I will never quit.

I will never leave a fallen comrade.

I am disciplined, physically and
mentally tough, trained and proficient
in my warrior tasks and drills.

I always maintain my arms,
my equipment and myself.

I am an expert and I am a professional.

I stand ready to deploy, engage,
and destroy the enemies of the
United States of America in close combat.

I am a guardian of freedom
and the American way of life.

I am an American Soldier.

The Army Civilian Creed

I am an Army Civilian—
a member of the Army team.

I am dedicated to our Army,
our Soldiers and Civilians.

I will always support the mission.

I provide stability and continuity
during war and peace.

I support and defend the Constitution of
the United States and consider it an
honor to serve our Nation and our Army.

I live the Army values of loyalty,
duty, respect, selfless service, honor,
integrity, and personal courage.

I am an Army Civilian.

Foreword

This capstone doctrine publication frames how we, as the Soldiers and Civilians of the United States Army, think about the strategic environment, develop and refine doctrine, and chart a course into the future. It is my vision of how the world has changed and how we as an Army will adapt to those changes, ensuring that we remain the world's dominant land force and a crucial contributor to the joint team. A key component of the way ahead is remaining focused on the professionalism of our force. Our Army Values are the essence of who we are, and those values rely on a bedrock of mutual trust among Soldiers, leaders, Families, and the American people that we serve.

Over the past 237 years, the United States Army has proudly served the Nation by winning its wars and securing the peace. Our history is marked by decisive action in a wide range of missions—including regular and irregular warfare, humanitarian assistance operations, engagement with allies, and support to civil authorities.

Today, our Army is entering not only a period of transition, but also great opportunity. The strategic environment has grown increasingly complex. Technological advances have created new ways to communicate with, to understand, and to influence others. Technology also empowers a much wider range of actors we must consider and interact with, to include those that come together virtually in cyberspace, unbounded by physical geography. At the same time, a decade of war has reinforced timeless lessons about the centrality of human beings in all aspects of military operations. We must build on these insights to change how we think about, plan for, and conduct all of our operations.

Although some will argue that technology will simplify future military operations, the evidence overwhelmingly indicates that warfare remains a fundamentally human endeavor. Direct engagement with people has always been, and remains, a core strength of the United States Army. We must recognize and fully embrace the changes in the environment that offer us new avenues to maintain our preeminence.

As part of the joint force, the United States Army ensures mission accomplishment, guarantees national security interests, compels adversaries, prosecutes military campaigns, and delivers lasting strategic results. It is what the American people expect and what our Nation's continued freedom demands. Warfighting is our primary mission. Everything that we do should be grounded in this fundamental principle. We must be responsive to combatant commanders as part of the joint force, rapidly dominating any operational environment across the range of military operations.

While we cannot predict the future, we can be certain that our Nation will continue to call on America's Army. Going forward, we will be an Army in transition. An Army that will apply the lessons learned in recent combat as we prepare for evolving threats. An Army that remains adaptive, innovative, versatile and ready as part of Joint Force 2020.

RAYMOND T. ODIERNO
General, United States Army
Chief of Staff

Change No. 1

ADP 1, C1

Headquarters
Department of the Army
Washington, DC, 7 November 2012

The Army

1. This change replaces paragraph 2-26 and 2-27.

2. A plus sign (+) marks new material.

3. ADP 1, 17 September 2012, is changed as follows:

Remove Old Pages	Insert New Pages
pages 2-9 and 2-10	pages 2-9 and 2-10

4. File this transmittal sheet in front of the publication for reference purposes.

By order of the Secretary of the Army:

RAYMOND T. ODIERNO
General, United States Army
Chief of Staff

Official:

JOYCE E. MORROW
Administrative Assistant to the
Secretary of the Army
1229701

DISTRIBUTION:
Active Army, Army National Guard, and United States Army Reserve: To be distributed in accordance with the initial distribution number (IDN) 110510, requirements for ADP 1.

Army Doctrine Publication
No. 1

Headquarters
Department of the Army
Washington, DC, 17 September 2012

The Army

Contents

DISTRIBUTION RESTRICTION: Approved for public release; distribution is unlimited.

*This publication supersedes FM 1, 14 June 2005.

Figures

Tables

Preface

Army Doctrine Publication (ADP) 1 is prepared under the direction of the Chief of Staff of the Army and is his vision for the Army. It states what the Army is, what the Army does, how the Army does it, and where the Army is going. It establishes the Army's contribution to America's landpower. ADP 1 delineates the Army's mission, purpose, and roles, deriving them from the Constitution; the Congress, in Title 10, United States Code; and the Department of Defense, in Department of Defense Directive 5100.01.

Army doctrine supports and is consistent with joint doctrine. This publication connects Army doctrine to joint doctrine as expressed in the relevant joint publications, especially Joint Publication (JP) 1, *Doctrine for the Armed Forces of the United States*, and JP 3-0, *Joint Operations*. ADP 1 also links the National Security, National Defense, and National Military Strategies with the Army's operational doctrine in ADP 3-0.

The principal audience of ADP 1 includes combatant commanders, other Services, all serving Soldiers, and all Army Civilians.

All photographs in this publication are from Department of Defense photographic archives available online at DefenseImagery.mil and associated Army Web pages.

ADP 1 implements the standardization agreement entitled Allied Joint Publication (AJP)-01, *Allied Joint Doctrine.*

ADP 1 uses joint terms where applicable. For terms and their definitions in the text, the term is italicized and the number of the proponent publication follows the definition.

ADP 1 applies to the Active Army, Army National Guard/Army National Guard of the United States, and United States Army Reserve unless otherwise stated.

United States Army Combined Arms Center is the proponent for this publication. The preparing agency is the Combined Arms Doctrine Directorate, United States Army Combined Arms Center. Send written comments and recommendations on a DA Form 2028 (*Recommended Changes to Publications and Blank Forms*) to Commander, U.S. Army Combined Arms Center and Fort Leavenworth, ATTN: ATZL-MCK-D (ADP 1), 300 McPherson Avenue, Fort Leavenworth, KS 66027-2337; by e-mail to usarmy.leavenworth.mccoe.mbx.cadd-org-mailbox@mail.mil; or submit an electronic DA Form 2028.

ACKNOWLEDGEMENTS

The TeachingAmericanHistory.org has granted permission to reproduce material from President George Washington's first annual address to Congress. Available at http://teachingamericanhistory.org/.TeachingAmericanHistory.org is a project of the Ashbrook Center at Ashland University.

Assorted photos from http://www.flickr.com/photos/soldiersmediacenter are courtesy of the United States Army.

Assorted photos from http://www.DefenseImagery.mil are courtesy of the United States Army.

Introduction

During the first year of the American Revolution, on 14 June 1775, the Second Continental Congress established "the American Continental Army." The United States Army is the senior Service of the Armed Forces. As one of the oldest American institutions, it predates the Declaration of Independence and the Constitution. For almost two and a half centuries, Army forces have protected the Nation. Our Army flag is adorned with over 180 campaign and battle streamers, each one signifying great sacrifices on behalf of the Nation. Because of the Army, the United States is independent and one undivided nation. The Army explored the Louisiana Purchase, ended slavery on the battlefields of the Civil War, helped build the Panama Canal, played a major part in winning two world wars, stood watch throughout the Cold War, deposed Saddam Hussein, and took the fight to Al Qaeda.

Introductory Figure. Soldiers—the strength of the nation

What does the uniform of the Army represent? For Soldiers it means that they have become part of something far bigger than themselves, a chance to serve their country and to change the world. It also means danger, long separations, grinding fatigue, and stress. Soldiers embrace the Soldier's Creed and Warrior Ethos (see the inside cover). For Army families, the uniform is a source of both pride and anxiety, knowing the sacrifices ahead. For our veterans, it represents one of the most important periods of their lives, pride in awards and decorations, and sometimes intense emotional and physical distress. For Army Civilians, Soldiers are the reason for their service. For the American citizen, Soldiers represent patriotism and selfless service, men and women in whom the Nation takes collective pride.

People around the world recognize the American Soldier as a symbol of the United States just as they do the White House or the Washington Monument. To American citizens, Soldiers are their sons, daughters, relatives, neighbors, and during disaster, their lifeline. To the Nation's allies, their presence signals an American commitment during a crisis. To potential enemies of the U.S., American Soldiers represent our means to seize and hold their vital territory, control populations and resources, and deliver the decisive blow. To U.S. enemies, Soldiers impose a lethal dilemma; Soldiers complement American air and maritime power by overcoming the protective effects of terrain, weather, and noncombatants.

Each day, young Americans volunteer to serve the Nation as Soldiers. Each day, Soldiers reenlist, continuing their service to the Nation despite being in some of the most dangerous places on earth. Their reasons for serving vary as much as their ethnicity, gender, and beliefs vary. Their diversity becomes our strength because they all share a common commitment to the United States, formalized in the oath they take upon beginning or continuing their service:

> *I, _____, do solemnly swear (or affirm) that I will support and defend the Constitution of the United States against all enemies, foreign and domestic; that I will bear true faith and allegiance to the same; and that I will obey the orders of the President of the United States and the orders of the officers appointed over me, according to regulations and the Uniform Code of Military Justice. So help me God.*

Through this oath, Soldiers affirm subordination to the Nation's elected civilian leadership and abstain from public political involvement. Soldiers voluntarily give up freedoms fellow citizens take for granted and become subject to military discipline and regulations. Soldiers accept unlimited liability in the service of our Nation. This becomes the foundation of our profession.

Soldiers require the support of the Army Civilian Corps. Army Civilians are professionals who provide long-term continuity and important skills needed away from the battlefield. They also take an oath to uphold and defend the Constitution. Although they are not subject to military discipline, they share the Army Values and follow the Army Civilian Creed (see the inside page) that echoes the Soldier's Creed.

Through our service, we continue the heritage of American Soldiers stretching back to the minutemen at Lexington and Concord. We stand with the continental line at Yorktown, charge with the Union regiments at Missionary Ridge, and go over the top in the Argonne Forest with the doughboys. We dig in with GIs to stop German armor in the Ardennes; board Huey helicopters with the grunts in Southeast Asia, and sweat in our body armor and Kevlar helmets while patrolling the hills of Afghanistan. Army Civilians support us, ensuring that our needs are met, our equipment is ready, and our facilities are first rate. Today, as in 1775, we are the strength of our Nation and its force of decisive action.

Chapter 1

Our Service

...[T]he United States Army remains the most agile, adaptable and capable force in the world. Ours is an Army that reflects America's diversity and represents the time-honored values that built our Nation—hard work, duty, selflessness, determination, honor and compassion.

2012 Army Posture Statement

U.S. forces operate in the air, land, maritime, space, and cyberspace domains. The land domain is the most complex of the domains, because it addresses humanity—its cultures, ethnicities, religions, and politics. War begins and ends based upon how it affects the land domain. Air, maritime, space, and cybernetic power affect the land domain indirectly; landpower is usually the arbiter of victory. The Army provides the United States with the landpower to prevent, shape, and win in the land domain. U.S. law, Department of Defense directives, and the nature of landpower mold the Army's mission.

THE LAND DOMAIN

1-1. The distinguishing characteristic of the land domain is the presence of humans in large numbers. Humans are interlopers in the air, on the sea, and in space; temporary occupants, maintained there through various technologies. Cyberspace is a technological repository and means of transit for information, but its content originates with people on land. Humans live on the land and affect almost every aspect of land operations. Soldiers operate among populations, not adjacent to them or above them. They accomplish missions face-to-face with people, in the midst of environmental, societal, religious, and political tumult. Winning battles and engagements is important but alone is usually insufficient to produce lasting change in the conditions that spawned conflict. Our effectiveness depends on our ability to manage populations and civilian authorities as much as it does on technical competence employing equipment. Managing populations before, during, and after all phases of the campaign normally determines its success or failure. Soldiers often cooperate, shape, influence, assist, and coerce according to the situation, varying their actions to make permanent the otherwise temporary gains achieved through combat.

1-2. The influence Soldiers exert before and after campaigns—shaping—is more important than ever. Shaping is best understood as altering conditions that, if left unchanged, can precipitate international crisis or war. Geographic combatant commanders shape their regions through many cooperative actions with partner nations.

The equipment, training, and financial assistance the United States provides to partner nations improve their abilities to secure themselves. This assistance often improves access to key regions. Security cooperation also communicates our position to potential adversaries in that region. If necessary, combat-ready Army units can deploy to threatened areas, reinforcing host-nation forces, complementing American air and sea power, and communicating unmistakable American intent to partner and adversary alike. These are the tangible effects of the Army's role in security cooperation and assistance. Other benefits are less tangible; these develop through face-to-face training involving our Soldiers and those of our partners. Working together develops trust between military partners. The impression we make upon multinational forces, local leaders, and other government agencies can produce lasting benefits.

1-3.   Few nations can afford a potent air force or navy; their principal military force is an army. This is true even in the Pacific littoral, a region with many large armies and only a few naval powers. For most nations, even in the Pacific region, their long-term security requirements stress land forces. Hence, U.S. strategic interests may be best met by extending American air, sea, and space power across the globe while working directly with multinational partners to improve their land forces. Our Soldiers form the most dominant landpower in the world, and this gives us unmatched credibility.

LAND OPERATIONS

1-4.   Land combat against an armed adversary is an intense, lethal human activity. Its conditions include complexity, chaos, fear, violence, fatigue, and uncertainty. The battlefield often teems with noncombatants and is crowded with infrastructure. In any conflict, Soldiers potentially face regular, irregular, or paramilitary enemy forces that possess advanced weapons and rapidly communicate using cellular devices. Our enemies will employ terror, criminal activity, and every means of messaging to further complicate our tasks. To an ever-increasing degree, activities in cyberspace and the information environment are inseparable from ground operations. Successful land combat requires protected friendly networks (wired and wireless) while exploiting or degrading the enemy's networks. The information environment, our use of it, and inform and influence activities continues to increase. Because the land environment is so complex, the potential for unintended consequences remains quite high. In the end, it is not the quality of weapons, but the quality of Soldiers employing them that determines mission success.

1-5.   Any mission can rapidly become a combination of combat, governance, and civil security. Most of our missions require combinations of lethal and nonlethal actions. This is inherent in the nature of land operations, usually conducted in the midst of noncombatants. When called upon, Soldiers accomplish nonlethal missions such as disaster relief and humanitarian assistance quickly and effectively. Regardless, our combat capability often underwrites our ability to provide assistance. Nobody in or outside the military profession should mistake the Army for anything other than a force organized, equipped, and trained for winning the Nation's wars.

1-6.   *Unified Land Operations* is the title of the Army's basic operational doctrine, ADP 3-0. It emphasizes the necessity of synchronizing our capabilities with the other Services (joint), other government agencies (interagency), other international government partners (intergovernmental), and military forces from partner nations (multinational). The basic premise of unified land operations is that Army forces combine offensive tasks, defensive tasks, stability tasks, and defense support of civil authorities (DSCA) in concert with joint, interagency, intergovernmental, and multinational partners. Army operations conducted overseas combine offensive, defensive, and stability tasks. Within the United States, we support civil authorities through DSCA. If hostile powers threaten the homeland, we combine defensive and offensive tasks with DSCA. The effort accorded to each task is proportional to the mission and varies with the situation. We label these combinations *decisive action* because of their necessity in any campaign.

Figure 1-1. The environment of land operations

1-7. Civilian agencies of the United States Government are indispensable partners with landpower. These agencies operate on land and depend on landpower to create secure conditions in regions of conflict. Secure land areas allow them to work directly with local leaders to address the causes of conflict. The enemy often perceives the Army's constructive actions in concert with these agencies as a significant threat, since we help isolate the enemy from popular support. In turn, the Army needs civilian agencies to provide expertise and resources needed to reconstruct facilities within war-torn regions and relieve Soldiers of the responsibility of administering to noncombatants.

LANDPOWER FOR THE NATION

1-8.   The Army gives the United States landpower. *Landpower* is the ability—by threat, force, or occupation—to gain, sustain, and exploit control over land, resources, and people (ADRP 3-0). Landpower includes the ability to—

- Impose the Nation's will on an enemy, by force if necessary.
- Engage to influence, shape, prevent, and deter in any operational environment.
- Establish and maintain a stable environment that sets the conditions for political and economic development.
- Address the consequences of catastrophic events—both natural and man-made—to restore infrastructure and reestablish basic civil services.
- Secure and support bases from which joint forces can influence and dominate the air, land, and maritime domains of an operational environment.

1-9.   No major conflict has ever been won without boots on the ground. Strategic change rarely stems from a single, rapid strike, and swift and victorious campaigns have been the exception in history. Often conflicts last months or years and become something quite different from the original plan. Campaigns require steady pressure exerted by U.S. military forces and those of partner nations, while working closely with civilian agencies. Soldiers not only seize, occupy, and defend land areas; they can also remain in the region until they secure the Nation's long-term strategic objectives. Indeed, inserting ground troops is the most tangible and durable measure of America's commitment to defend American interests. It signals the Nation's intent to protect friends and deny aggression.

Figure 1-2. Landpower makes permanent the temporary effects of battle

OUR ROLES: PREVENT, SHAPE, AND WIN

The Army is globally engaged and regionally responsive; it is an indispensible partner and provider of a full range of capabilities to Combatant Commanders in a Joint, Interagency, Intergovernmental, and Multi-national (JIIM) environment. As part of the Joint Force and as America's Army, in all that we offer, we guarantee the agility, versatility and depth to Prevent, Shape and Win.

The Army Vision

1-10. The Army Vision captures the three strategic roles of the Army: prevent, shape, and win. We derive our roles from the National Military Strategy and Department of Defense directives. Our roles clarify the enduring reasons for which the Army is manned, trained, and equipped.

PREVENT

1-11. First, the Army must prevent conflict. Prevention requires a credible force. Friends and adversaries must believe that the Army is credible in order to prevent conflicts. Credibility equates to capability and is built upon combat-ready forces that can be tailored and deployed rapidly. Credible Army forces convince potential opponents that, committed as part of our joint force, the U.S. Army is unbeatable. Partner nations under external threat need to understand that introducing U.S. forces alters the regional military balance in their favor and bolsters their resolve to resist aggression.

1-12. Credible Army forces reduce the risk of miscalculation by an adversary. We cannot depend upon our reputation alone to dissuade our adversaries. They must understand what we can do today and tomorrow, in a way that leaves no room for miscalculation. To convince any potential adversary, we need rigorous and realistic training, expert leaders, modern equipment, and quality personnel. Given that, our landpower becomes more than credible; combined with the Nation's air, sea, and space-based power, it becomes preeminent.

SHAPE

1-13. Second, the Army must help shape the international environment to enable our partners and contain our enemies. We do that by engaging with partners, fostering mutual understanding through military-to-military contacts, and helping partners build the capacity to defend themselves. Shaping the strategic security environment improves the chance for peace around the world. It diminishes regional tensions and is therefore vital to American security interests. Each geographic combatant commander develops programs to improve regional stability and promote peace through security cooperation. American military capabilities can reassure allies, while dissuading adversaries. Shaping by itself cannot prevent conflict, but it nudges global regions away from military confrontation and increases the effect of diplomatic, informational, and economic instruments of national power.

1-14. Soldiers are particularly important in this effort, since all nations have land security elements, even if lacking credible air and naval forces. To the degree that other nations see us as the best army in the world, they gravitate to us to help them achieve the same high standards of military performance, or tie their security to the world's most capable army. Soldiers deploy around the world to train with security forces of other nations. Army special operations forces carry out a significant part of this effort; however, conventional units frequently train with foreign counterparts. Concurrently, our Soldiers and Army Civilians train foreign military personnel at Army bases. This unobtrusive use of landpower quietly builds multinational partnerships that may be critical in war. It increases our partners' capacities to provide for their own defense and is vital to ensuring we have access to regional bases should Army forces have to deploy to their region.

Figure 1-3. American Soldiers training with Croatian forces

WIN

1-15. Finally, the Army must be ready to win, and win decisively. We must be able to attack and defend successfully against enemy ground forces. Joint force commanders require Army units that can destroy an enemy with all types of combat power. Land combat remains chaotic, lethal, and intensely human. The ability to prevail in ground combat becomes a decisive factor in breaking the enemy's will. If the enemy cannot be defeated from a distance using Army and joint capabilities, then Soldiers close with and destroy the enemy—room to room, face to face. This requires skilled use of combined arms, the ability to fight using all available combat power in complementary ways. Combined arms multiply the effectiveness of Army units exponentially. If Army units cannot find, fix, close with, and destroy armed opponents in any terrain; exploit success; shatter opponents' coherence; and break the enemy's will to continue the fight, then neither we, nor the joint force, will be decisive. But lethality, by itself, is not enough. If Army forces do not address the requirements of noncombatants in the joint operational area before, during, and after battle, then the tactical victories achieved by our firepower only lead to strategic failure and world condemnation.

1-16. For the Army, winning is especially important because historically, we commit the greatest number of personnel to the combat area and suffer the highest casualties. With so much at stake, the American people expect our commanders to advise political leaders candidly on the military implications of any potential conflict beforehand. If U.S. forces fight, the Nation expects us to inflict a defeat of sufficient magnitude that the enemy abandons his objectives and agrees to peace on our terms. In other words, Americans expect us to dominate and win decisively.

1-17. Prevent, shape, and win summarizes the Army's roles as part of the joint force. Our roles depend upon our capabilities, depth, experience, and professionalism. Preventing and shaping are not episodic. We fulfill these roles continuously, based upon the requirements of combatant commanders. When the Army is committed, winning is our non-negotiable obligation to the Nation. When we combine our capabilities with Marines, sailors, and airmen, the United States is the greatest military power on earth. As we, the Army, continue to adapt to future strategic challenges, we remember that we are the force of decisive action; we are the landpower required by the Nation to prevent, shape, and win.

THE ARMY MISSION

1-18. We derive our mission from the intent of Congress and through the laws governing the Armed Forces. The Constitution of the United States gives Congress the authority to determine the size and organization of the Army, and gives the President overall command of the Armed Forces. Title 10, United States Code (USC), regulates the Armed Forces. In Title 10, USC, Congress specifies its intent and requirements for the Army:

> *(a) It is the intent of Congress to provide an Army that is capable, in conjunction with the other armed forces, of (1) preserving the peace and security, and providing for the defense, of the United States, the Commonwealths and possessions, and any areas occupied by the United States; (2) supporting the national policies; (3) implementing the national objectives; and (4) overcoming any nations responsible for aggressive acts that imperil the peace and security of the United States.*

> *(b) In general, the Army, within the Department of the Army, includes land combat and service forces and such aviation and water transport as may be organic therein. **It shall be organized, trained, and equipped primarily for prompt and sustained combat incident to operations on land** [emphasis added]. It is responsible for the preparation of land forces necessary for the effective prosecution of war except as otherwise assigned and, in accordance with integrated*

joint mobilization plans, for the expansion of the peacetime components of the Army to meet the needs of war.

1-19. Army forces fight on land as part of an integrated joint force and conduct "prompt and sustained" combined arms maneuver. "Prompt" requires us to provide combat-ready forces immediately; "sustained" requires us to maintain Army forces in the fight until the President says otherwise. Therefore, the forces we provide require the endurance to continue the fight indefinitely.

1-20. We refine our mission based on Department of Defense Directive 5100.01. This directive assigns specific responsibilities to the Armed Forces. In common with all of the Services, the Army provides "conventional, strategic, and special operations forces to conduct the range of operations as defined by the President and the Secretary of Defense." This directive specifically charges us to "...organize, train, equip, and provide forces with expeditionary and campaign qualities" in order to—

- Conduct operations in all environments and types of terrain, including complex urban environments, to defeat enemy ground forces, and seize, occupy, and defend land areas.
- Conduct air and missile defense to support joint campaigns and assist in achieving air superiority.
- Conduct airborne, air assault, and amphibious operations.
- Occupy territories abroad and provide for the initial establishment of a military government pending transfer of this responsibility to another authority.
- Interdict enemy air, sea, and space forces and [their lines of] communications through operations on or from the land.
- Provide logistics to joint operations and campaigns, including joint over-the-shore and intra-theater transport of time-sensitive, mission-critical personnel and materiel.
- Conduct authorized civil works programs and other civil activities prescribed by law.

1-21. Based upon Title 10, USC, and Department of Defense Directive 5100.01, the Army's mission becomes:

The United States Army Mission

The mission of the United States Army is to fight and win the Nation's wars through prompt and sustained land combat, as part of the joint force. We do this by—

Organizing, equipping, and training Army forces for prompt and sustained combat incident to operations on land;

Integrating our capabilities with those of the other Armed Services;

Accomplishing all missions assigned by the President, Secretary of Defense, and combatant commanders;

Remaining ready while preparing for the future.

Chapter 2

Our Profession

[We will] foster continued commitment to the Army Profession, a noble and selfless calling founded on the bedrock of trust.

Chief of Staff of the Army Marching Orders

The Army has a dual nature—it is both a military department (a part of the Armed Forces) and a military profession. As one of the Nation's armed services, we carry out the missions assigned to us by the Commander in Chief in accordance with the law and intent of Congress. As a unique military profession, the Army is built upon an ethos of trust, which buttresses four other essential characteristics of our profession: military expertise, honorable service, esprit de corps, and stewardship. *The Army Profession: 2012, After More than a Decade of Conflict* provides an in-depth review of Army professional responsibilities.

Figure 2-1. "Thumbs up!"—a profession built on trust

A PROFESSION BUILT ON TRUST

2-1.   Trust is "assured reliance on the character, ability, strength, or truth of someone or something." It is the essence of being an effective Soldier. Trust is the core intangible needed by the Army inside and outside the profession. Our ability to fulfill our strategic roles and discharge our responsibilities to the Nation depends upon trust between Soldiers; between Soldiers and their leaders; among Soldiers, their families, and the Army; and between the Army and the Nation. Ultimately, the Nation trusts the Army to provide landpower when, where, and how combatant commanders need it.

TRUST BETWEEN SOLDIERS

2-2.   In battle, Soldiers primarily fight for one another, not just for their country or some ideal. Heroism is not the action of naturally brave men and women; it originates in the bonds between Soldiers and their commitment to each other. This impels them to overcome paralyzing fear because they will not let their comrades down. They entrust their lives to the Soldiers on their left and right, and focus on doing their duty in a way that maintains the trust of their comrades. Without this level of trust, there is no cohesion, no ability to stand fast in the most horrific environments. The level of resilience and cohesion within an Army unit correlates directly to trust between Soldiers in that unit.

2-3.   Building trust in an Army as diverse as ours begins with developing common values—the Army values shown in figure 2-2—in each Soldier. Trust begins as Soldiers enter the service and is reinforced throughout the period of their service. The Army Values become the catalyst to developing the trust between Soldiers, and these values instill traits needed not only in war but for the remainder of their lives. (Further discussion on the Army Values is contained in ADRP 6-22.)

TRUST BETWEEN SOLDIERS AND LEADERS

2-4.   Trust between Soldiers binds individuals into resilient units, but it cannot accomplish missions nor generate high levels of unit effectiveness. That comes from the trust that Soldiers have with their leaders. Trust between a superior and a subordinate is the second critical aspect of trust; without it, Soldiers will not follow orders except from fear of consequences. Consider the choice our Soldiers make when the likely consequences of following an order (death or wounding) exceed the legal consequences of disobeying it (courts martial). Their collective decision to obey orders is the difference between mission accomplishment and failure. This is based primarily on their trust in their leaders. Accordingly, our doctrine emphasizes building trust up and down the chain of command. Mission command, our fundamental doctrine for command, requires trust throughout the chain of command. Superiors trust subordinates and empower them to accomplish missions within their intent. Subordinates trust superiors to give them the freedom to execute the commander's intent and support their decisions. The trust between all levels depends upon candor.

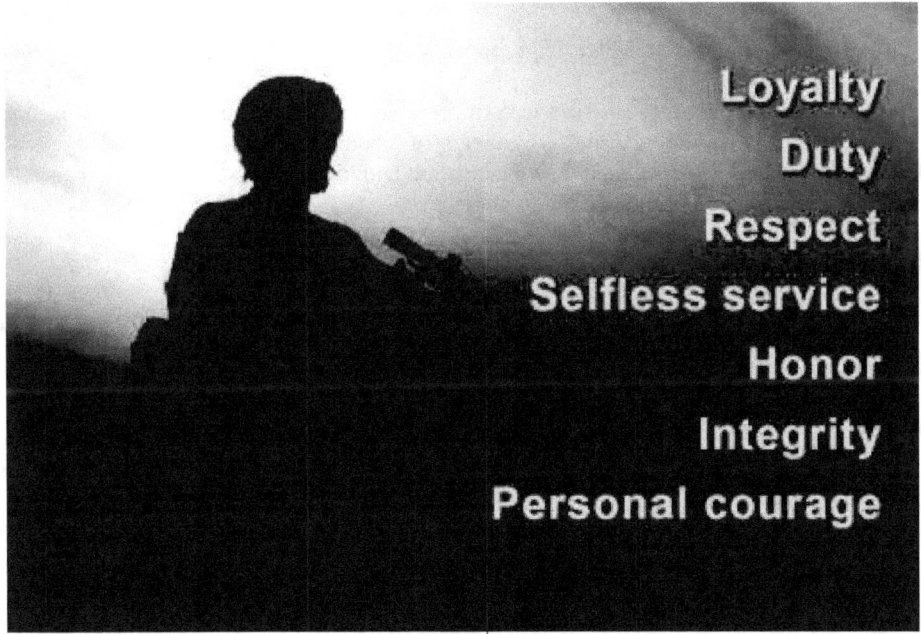

Figure 2-2. The Army Values

TRUST AMONG SOLDIERS, THEIR FAMILIES, AND THE ARMY

2-5. Beneath the uniform, Soldiers are people with similar priorities to other Americans. Many things inspire a Soldier to join the Army, but families usually keep professional Soldiers in the Army. The Army is committed to Soldiers and their families, providing a strong, supportive environment that enhances their strength and resilience. The trust between the Army and our Soldiers' families is essential to preserving an all-volunteer force. We ask much of our Soldiers and their families. In return, we need to provide a quality of life commensurate with the Soldier's service to the Nation.

TRUST BETWEEN THE ARMY AND THE AMERICAN PEOPLE

2-6. The Army is among the institutions held in highest confidence by Americans. Trust underwrites our relationship to the Nation and the citizens we protect. Without the confidence of the citizens, we could not maintain the all-volunteer force. Without the confidence of the President and Congress, we could not maintain the readiness required to fight and win.

2-7. Soldiers swear an oath to the Constitution, and do so freely, without compulsion or reservation. Americans place special trust and confidence in Soldiers to serve the Nation before all other considerations. In return, Soldiers ask that their follow citizens remember their sacrifice, not with tangible rewards, but with respect and appreciation for having done their duty.

MILITARY EXPERTISE

2-8.   Like other professions, we are a repository of a unique body of knowledge—in our case, the employment of landpower in a distinctly American military context. The context is distinct because of American military structure and the way the U.S. military employs joint capabilities. Also like other professions, we apply our knowledge using expertise developed through extensive education and training. Like other professions, we certify individual and organizational competence.

FIELDS OF PROFESSIONAL KNOWLEDGE

2-9.   We develop and maintain professional knowledge in four broad fields. First, the *military-technical* field encompasses the doctrine of how the Army applies landpower, including the integration and adaptation of technology, the organization of units, and the planning and execution of military operations. Second, the *moral-ethical* field describes how the Army applies its combat power according to law and the expectation of our citizens. Third, the *political-cultural* field prescribes how personnel and units operate effectively across and outside the Army's institutional boundaries. Land operations require cooperation with other Armed Forces, foreign militaries, other government agencies (our own and those of other countries), and all manner of human societies. Finally, the Army specializes in *leader development* because good leaders are the qualitative multiplier on any battlefield, the most dynamic element of combat power.

2-10. We impart our professional knowledge through training and education at both individual and unit levels. Doctrine expresses a common body of knowledge that Soldiers and Army Civilians use to educate and train. Individual education maintains professional knowledge across generations. Individual and unit training transform knowledge into expertise—a high level of skill in applying knowledge in actual situations.

2-11. Army doctrine stresses mission command, the conduct of military operations that allows subordinate leaders maximum initiative. It acknowledges that operations in the land domain are complex and often chaotic, and micro-management does not work. Mission command emphasizes competent leaders applying their expertise to the situation as it exists on the ground and accomplishing the mission based on their commander's intent. Mission command fosters a culture of trust, mutual understanding, and a willingness to learn from mistakes.

2-12. Training does more than develop technical expertise. It encourages Army leaders to exercise discretionary judgments without close supervision. Given the nature of modern land operations, this ability is critically important because of the lethality of what we do. The failure of individual Army professionals to make the right decision can be devastating, particularly in an omnipresent information environment. The Army Values shape and bind Soldiers' and Army Civilians' discretionary judgments. We strive to ingrain a strong professional ethos, one of trust, honorable service, and high esprit de corps, in parallel with our technical expertise.

2-13. The Army certifies the expertise of individuals and units. Certification of individuals occurs at different stages during their service and varies based upon the particular skill set. The Army is a profession of professions, some uniquely military and others with close civilian counterparts. In the latter case, Army professionals first earn certification in their broader profession, for example as a doctor or lawyer. Initial certification may occur in a civil school, a military venue, or both. Soldiers and Army Civilians then develop further expertise based on specific military application, such as courts martial procedures for lawyers. However, military expertise is highly specialized and validated wholly within the Army. For example, training and validation of an artillery crewman has no civilian equivalent.

2-14. Three broad criteria apply to certification of Army professionals. Individuals develop certification in detail through Army branches, proponents, and Army Civilian career field programs. Certification measures competence, character, and commitment. For advancement, Army professionals demonstrate competence; their mastery of specific skills. Character ensures Army professionals use their expertise on behalf of the American people and only in accordance with the law. Commitment reflects each individual's willingness to put the requirements of the Army and Nation above their personal goals.

2-15. Units are also certified, but in terms of readiness to accomplish their missions. Unit compliance with safety and personnel regulations is measured through inspections. Unit combat readiness is determined by demonstrated performance in training events and through candid assessment by the chain of command. Units deploying to combat typically go through an additional phase of training called a mission rehearsal exercise that mimics likely missions as closely as safety, resources, and terrain allow.

MEMBERSHIP IN THE ARMY PROFESSION

2-16. The Army profession recognizes two communities of practice: the *Profession of Arms* and *Army Civilian Corps*. After taking an initial oath, each individual (military or civilian) becomes a member of the Army profession, but an individual is not a professional until certified. The transition from an aspiring professional to a professional in either community is not automatic. Initial certification occurs upon graduation or completion of the first qualifying event such as Advanced Individual Training for the Soldier. Membership is a status that is earned through certification and periodic recertification in competence, character, and commitment. Membership in the Army profession carries with it significant responsibility—the effective and ethical application of combat power. Additional certifications follow as the professional advances in skill, experience, and responsibility. The responsibility for each individual's development and certification is a mutual one, shared by the individual with the Army.

Figure 2-3. Initial certification—crewmen learn to operate the M1A1 tank

HONORABLE SERVICE

2-17. Official recognition of honorable service is the external manifestation of the Army professional's oath and ethical conduct. Selfless service is an internalized value that determines the character of their time in the Army. Our Soldiers and Army Civilians join to serve the Nation—to support and defend the Constitution and to do so in a way that upholds U.S. law and American values. Army professionals are duty-bound to uphold their oath, embody the Soldier's Creed and Army Civilian Creed, and instill the Army Values in themselves and others. This is our collective ethos—the moral principles that define our profession.

OUR CONSTITUTIONAL OATHS

2-18. Article VI of the Constitution requires that every member of the Army profession—military or civilian, officer or enlisted—"shall be bound by Oath or Affirmation, to support this Constitution." An oath is an individual moral commitment made publicly. The gravity of this commitment is that it binds Soldiers to an unlimited liability, acceptance of the risk of serious personal harm or death. This fact distinguishes the uniformed members of the Army from its Civilian Corps and all other employees of the Federal Government. This Constitutional oath is legally binding and makes Soldiers subject to the Uniform Code of Military Justice, federal laws applicable to the Armed Forces, and the Law of Land Warfare.

OUR ETHICS

2-19. All warfare challenges the morals and ethics of Soldiers. An enemy may not respect international conventions and may commit atrocities with the aim of provoking retaliation in kind. Any loss of discipline on the part of our Soldiers is then exploited in propaganda and magnified through the media. The ethical challenge rests heavily on small-unit leaders who maintain discipline and ensure that the conduct of Soldiers remains within ethical and moral boundaries. There are five compelling reasons for this. First, humane treatment of detainees encourages enemy surrender and thereby reduces friendly losses. Conversely, nothing emboldens enemy resistance like the belief that U.S. forces will kill or torture prisoners. Second, humane treatment of noncombatants reduces their antagonism toward U.S. forces and may lead to valuable intelligence. Third, leaders make decisions in action fraught with consequences. If leaders lack an ethical foundation, those consequences can adversely affect mission accomplishment. Fourth, leaders who tacitly accept misconduct, or far worse, encourage it, erode discipline within the unit. This destroys unit cohesion and esprit de corps. Finally, Soldiers must live with the consequences of their conduct. All leaders shoulder the responsibility that their subordinates return from a campaign not only as good Soldiers, but also as good citizens with pride in their service to the Nation. General Creighton Abrams, reflecting on his service spanning World War II, Korea, the Cold War, and Vietnam, stated it well: "While we are guarding the country, we must accept being the guardian of the finest ethics; the country needs it and we must do it."

ESPRIT DE CORPS

2-20. Fighting and winning requires professionals imbued with respect for our history and tradition and committed to the highest standards of individual and collective excellence. This respect and commitment is what we mean by esprit de corps. Professionals foster and sustain esprit de corps throughout the Army profession. Professionals exude purpose, demonstrate strong bonds of loyalty and pride, and place the mission above their own welfare. This makes us an Army family, one that takes care of its own and never leaves a fellow comrade or their family behind.

TRADITIONS AND HISTORY

2-21. Our esprit de corps is rooted in tradition and history. Very few American institutions have a history as rich or long as ours. We emphasize this through the practice of customs, traditions, and ceremonies. Units and organizations preserve their unit histories and display them in unit distinctive insignia (such as unit crests, patches, and mottos). These practices and symbols give us a sense of commitment, identify the cause we serve, and unite us to those who have gone before and sacrificed so much.

DISCIPLINE AND PRIDE

2-22. Discipline and pride are the hallmark of units with high esprit de corps. Discipline is behavior tempered by high standards of conduct and performance. Discipline reflects the self-control necessary in the face of temptation, obstacles, and adversity, and the fear to do the harder right instead of the easier wrong. Pride stems from an internalized recognition that obstacles, adversity, and fear can be mastered through discipline and teamwork. Discipline and pride go together with judgment, expertise, and experience to create military and civilian professionals.

Figure 2-4. Esprit de corps reflected in our customs and ceremonies

ESPRIT AT ALL LEVELS

2-23. Esprit de corps applies at all levels from the individual to the Army overall. Individual esprit shows in high motivation, discipline, and morale. Soldiers with esprit de corps have pride, a sense of accomplishment in doing a good job or seeing a subordinate develop, and shared values. A small-unit or team's esprit de corps is reflected through mission focus, technical and tactical proficiency, teamwork, and ultimately cohesion on the battlefield. At the large-unit or organizational level, esprit de corps reflects the shared commitment Army professionals have for the organization—its mission and goals, its traditions and customs, and its heritage of honorable service. It reflects the pride of being a "Marne Soldier" or a "Screaming Eagle." Unit and organizational esprit de corps is built on an open command climate of candor, trust, and respect, with leaders who exhibit concern for the welfare of subordinates and set the example for expertise and honorable service.

STEWARDSHIP

2-24. Stewardship reflects the Army professional's responsibilities to the Army and Nation. As professionals, we remain responsible for today's missions, even as we build a better Army for tomorrow. We ensure that our profession is capable of succeeding in whatever missions our Nation gives us in the future. Through stewardship, Army professionals commit to the long-term effectiveness of the profession.

2-25. To be an Army professional and a steward of the profession is not just a job, it is an office. The office Army professionals enter upon swearing the oath is not our physical workspace; it is our ethical workspace. The oaths taken by Army officers and Army Civilians conclude with "...and that I will well and faithfully discharge the duties of the *office* [emphasis added] upon which I am about to enter". Title 10, United States Code, contains our explicit responsibilities as cited in paragraph 1-18. We provide highly effective landpower for whatever purpose the Nation requires. In practical terms, our public accounting as a profession occurs when the Nation calls us to accomplish the Army mission: to fight and win our Nation's wars. Stewardship therefore involves a subordination of all Army leaders, civilian and military, to the larger responsibilities of the profession: being the stewards of the trust between the Army and American people.

CIVIL-MILITARY RELATIONS

+ 2-26. Military professionals also have a stewardship responsibility for the relationship between the military and civilian leadership of the Army. Civilian control of the military is embedded in our Constitution and serves as the cornerstone of our military. Military professionals understand this and appreciate the critical role this concept has played throughout our history. Equally important, this concept requires that military professionals understand the role of our civilian leaders and their responsibilities to the civilian leadership. Military professionals have unique expertise, and their input is vital to formulating and executing effective defense policy.

ARMY PROFESSIONALS AND THE NATION

+ 2-27. Army professionals have a dual charge. On the one hand, we Army professionals defend the Nation from danger by applying landpower when and where directed by civilian authority. On the other hand, we are also citizens whose strength of character exemplifies the ideals espoused by our ethos. By living our values, we extend the character of our profession far beyond active service.

This page intentionally left blank.

Chapter 3

The Army and the Joint Force

The synergy that results from the operations of joint forces maximizes the capability of the force. The advantage of a joint team extends beyond the battlefield and across the range of military operations.

JP 1

Landpower complements air, maritime, and space-based power, and in turn the other Services make the Army the preeminent ground force in the world. Joint interdependence is the evolution of combined arms; the use of a specific military capability to multiply the effectiveness and redress the shortcomings of another. Combined arms is not new idea, and mastery of combined arms has been crucial to our success from the Civil War onwards. But where combined arms are tactical in nature, joint interdependence is combined arms achieved at tactical, operational, and strategic levels.

JOINT MISSIONS

3-1. The current Defense Strategic Guidance specifies the "Primary Missions of the U.S. Armed Forces." These are reiterated in the *Army Strategic Planning Guidance*. Each mission requires applying conventional and special operations forces in conjunction with the other instruments of national power—diplomatic, economic, and informational. In all but one mission—maintain a nuclear deterrent—the Army is a vital contributor to the joint force. In several missions, landpower is decisive. The eleven missions are listed below:

- Counter terrorism and irregular warfare.
- Deter and defeat aggression.
- Project power despite anti-access/area denial challenges.
- Counter weapons of mass destruction.
- Operate effectively in cyberspace.
- Operate effectively in space.
- Maintain a safe, secure, and effective nuclear deterrent.
- Defend the homeland and provide support to civil authorities.
- Provide a stabilizing presence.
- Conduct stability and counterinsurgency operations.
- Conduct humanitarian, disaster relief, and other operations.

3-2. The *Army Strategic Planning Guidance* for 2012 reiterates these missions and states, "In all the mission areas the Army will consider joint interdependence as a best value solution." Joint interdependence is the deliberate reliance of one armed service on the capabilities of another armed service. The Army depends on the other Services for their specialized capabilities; likewise, those Services depend on Army capabilities. Army capabilities are extensive and diverse. They range from ballistic missile defense to capabilities such as ground transportation support, veterinary services, engineering, and food inspection. Collectively, the Army calls these capabilities "Army support to other Services." At the strategic level, the Department of Defense examines the capabilities of all the Services, and determines which capabilities each Service provides best. A significant change in the Armed Forces is a willingness by each Service to specialize in capabilities that that Service must accomplish while depending on the other Services for additional capabilities. This creates joint interdependence—an integration of complementary means at the tactical, operational, and strategic levels.

3-3. The Army gives the combatant commander depth and versatility because landpower expands the friendly range of military options. The Army, uniquely, provides a combination of armored, medium, light, and airborne forces. Along with a full suite of enablers, this allows us to provide tailorable and scalable force packages for various contingencies. By multiplying the range of U.S. capabilities that the adversary must counter, the Army narrows options that might otherwise work against a lesser opponent or a coalition partner supported only by U.S. air and maritime power.

3-4. Four of the primary missions of the Armed Forces require either the commitment of global response forces, ground forces in large numbers, or the ready availability of large numbers of Soldiers to address likely contingencies. Our major operating force headquarters support combatant commanders' planning for commitment of Army forces across the range of military operations. The Nation's leaders recognize the need for landpower in counter terrorism and irregular warfare; this priority mission of the Army has existed for more than a decade. Landpower deters aggression through perceived capability and presence. Stability and counterinsurgency operations require boots on the ground, if not American, often indigenous ground forces trained and supported by U.S. Soldiers. If war breaks out, landpower complements joint capability by confronting the enemy with a lethal dilemma involving air, land, and maritime powers. The defense of our homeland and support of civil authorities require the efforts of all the other Services. However, defense support of civil authorities is manpower intensive and depends on face-to-face support where American citizens live—on the ground.

3-5. America's security requirements are global; therefore, our ability to project military power depends upon access and forcible entry. Access is facilitated by the Army's ability to shape and assist host-nation forces with securing bases for American forces. Forcible entry may be required if an enemy denies access. The Army's parachute and air assault forces provide the joint force commander with flexible options to seize a lodgment or deceive the enemy. Weapons of mass destruction are the greatest threat to our homeland. Landpower is the only assured means of removing those weapons at their source if other measures are inadequate. As proven in Europe and Asia, U.S. Soldiers provide a stabilizing presence. Deployed Soldiers raise the ante against aggression and create the secure environment necessary for peaceful development. Humanitarian assistance and disaster relief, like support of civil authorities, usually prove manpower intensive. When necessary, Army specialists support international aid organizations. If the situation is dire, such as that following the Haiti earthquake, Soldiers supply disciplined manpower to assist the affected region directly.

3-6.   The Army is a major beneficiary of and contributor to joint capabilities in both cyberspace and space. Assured access to cyberspace increases combined arms performance and integrates it with joint capabilities. The Army disperses and maneuvers over vast areas, exerting the decisive effect of landpower with remarkably small numbers of Soldiers. However, cyberspace is now a battleground and the intensity of cyber electromagnetic activities continues to multiply. Similarly, U.S. forces cannot continue to plan on unimpeded support from space systems. Space systems allow the Army to employ weapons systems rapidly, lethally and discreetly. Adversaries understand the advantages the Army accrues from American space superiority and are actively developing means to deny space support to our Soldiers. Landpower can remove an enemy's access to space and cyberspace by seizing and occupying the locations from which the enemy operates space and cyber systems. At the same time, superior organization, training, and equipment prepares the Army to operate effectively despite degraded networks, intermittent communications, and intensive combat in space and cyberspace. This is why we stress mission command as both a critical function and a guiding philosophy.

3-7.   No better example of joint interdependence may be found than nuclear deterrence. At the end of the Cold War, the Army dismantled its tactical nuclear weapons and rolled the savings into conventional and special operations capabilities. Today the Army complements U.S. nuclear deterrent by providing ballistic missile and cruise missile defense capabilities necessary for nonnuclear operations.

CORE AND ENABLING COMPETENCIES

3-8.   The joint force commander asks for and receives Army forces based upon what they can do on the ground. The Army's indispensable contributions to the joint force — the core competencies — are combined arms maneuver and wide area security, as noted in ADP 3-0. But several vital capabilities — the enabling competencies — are fundamental to the Army's ability to maneuver and secure land areas for the joint force. These enabling competencies include security cooperation, tailoring forces, entry operations, flexible mission command, the support we provide to the joint force and

Core Competencies
- Combined arms maneuver
- Wide area security

Enabling Competencies
- Support security cooperation
- Tailor forces for the combatant commander
- Conduct entry operations
- Provide flexible mission command
- Support joint and Army Forces
- Support domestic civil authorities
- Mobilize and integrate the Reserve Components

ourselves, domestic support, and mobilizing Reserve Components. These capabilities are not an exclusive set; the other Services perform similar functions. Nor are these an exhaustive list of what the Army does at the tactical and operational levels.

COMBINED ARMS MANEUVER

3-9. The lethality of the battlefield demands mastery of combined arms—not just combinations of Army capabilities, but the full array of joint capabilities. The skills needed to synchronize joint firepower and land maneuver are at the apex of military proficiency. The ability to prevail in combined arms maneuver is a decisive factor in breaking the enemy's will.

3-10. Army forces find, fix, close with, and destroy enemy forces on land and then exploit opportunities created by the enemy's defeat. Maneuver places the enemy at a physical disadvantage; the enemy is more vulnerable to our weapons than Army forces are to the enemy's. In addition to physical disadvantages, maneuver imposes a psychological disadvantage on the enemy. Individual fear leads to a breakdown in unit cohesion. When the enemy's cohesion breaks, the enemy is routed and destroyed in detail. If long range weapons cannot destroy or dislodge the enemy, Soldiers move in on the enemy until there is no longer any escape. The enemy then surrenders, flees in disorder, or dies.

3-11. Combined arms maneuver encompasses the tactical tasks associated with offensive and defensive operations, security operations such a screen or guard mission, reconnaissance missions, and special purpose tasks such as river crossings. Nothing the Army does is as challenging as combined arms maneuver.

WIDE AREA SECURITY

3-12. Wide area security is the ability of landpower to secure and control populations, resources, and terrain within a joint operational area. It can be highly cooperative, such as the integration of Army units in a host nation under threat from hostile power. It can be coercive, as when Army forces seize a lodgment and enforce security and control over populated areas within the lodgment. It can be a carefully balanced mix of coercive and cooperative actions, typical in counterinsurgency operations.

3-13. Stability operations are the tactical tasks that the Army conducts to improve conditions for noncombatants within areas of operations outside the United States. Basic tasks include providing security, exercising control, and providing life-sustaining support, such as food and water. More complex tasks may include governance and economic development. Wherever possible, stability operations involve the host-nation government and security forces. Stability operations are an indispensable complement to offensive and defensive operations.

SUPPORT SECURITY COOPERATION

3-14. Shaping the security environment diminishes regional tensions and is vital to the Nation. Each geographic combatant commander develops programs to improve regional stability and promote peace through security cooperation. The theater army provides an important link to resources necessary to implement the combatant commander's theater strategy; therefore, combatant commanders rely heavily on the theater army to execute security cooperation missions. American military capabilities can reassure allies and partners, build trust and confidence, and deter aggression. Soldiers are particularly important in security cooperation since all nations—even if they lack air and naval forces—have land-based security elements. U.S. Soldiers deploy around the world to train with security forces of other nations. Army special forces carry out a significant part of this effort; however, larger Army units frequently train with foreign counterparts.

TAILOR FORCES FOR THE COMBATANT COMMANDER

3-15. ADRP 3-0 defines *force tailoring* as the process of determining the right mix of forces and the sequence of their deployment in support of a joint force commander. Force tailoring is an ability to translate the combatant commanders' requirements for landpower into force packages of Army units, ready for deployment to the joint operational area and employment upon arrival. The Army's wide array of capabilities means joint force commanders request and the Army provides landpower organized for any mix of tasks, from all-out combat to humanitarian assistance. Our diverse capabilities allow us to augment the other Services with unique Army specialties, even when large numbers of troops are not needed. In practice, force tailoring is an immensely complex undertaking that drives manning, organization, training, and readiness; in short, almost everything we do before Soldiers arrive on the battlefield.

3-16. Landpower provides the joint force commander with depth and versatility, not just in campaigns, but before and after combat operations. The Army maintains a shaping presence in combatant commands through regional alignment of units and headquarters. Regionally aligned forces adapt their training and planning to likely contingencies in a particular area of responsibility. Regional alignment builds familiarity between multinational partners and improves the Army's ability to respond in a crisis.

CONDUCT ENTRY OPERATIONS

3-17. The Army trains and equips combat forces to conduct airborne (parachute) and air assault (helicopter) operations to seize lodgments or other key objectives. Joint forcible entry forces an enemy to defend against numerous joint options and gives the joint force commander the initiative. In some instances, the enemy may not oppose the deployment, but conditions may be primitive enough that a protected lodgment is crucial. As soon as initial entry forces secure the lodgment, the joint force commander introduces other forces, such as additional maneuver forces, air assets, and special operations forces, to exploit the situation from the bases seized by assault or occupation. The Army provides much of the theater opening capability within the lodgment. Army forces deploy some of this capability from outside the region while Army logisticians and transportation experts contract and organize it as soon as conditions permit.

Figure 3-1. Combined arms maneuver

PROVIDE FLEXIBLE MISSION COMMAND

3-18. Mission command encompasses the art of command and the science of control. It is commander-centric. Command is much more than authority. Authority is the legal basis for command, but having authority and using it effectively is an art. Even a relatively small Army formation such as a battalion has dozens of organizations doing a myriad of tasks. When combat adds in fear, fatigue, and chance, leaders must balance authority and leadership. Land operations depend on human qualities such as trust, belief, confidence, and perseverance. In conditions of great stress, commanders apply the necessary balance of qualities to get their units to accomplish the mission. Because of the complexity of land operations, we stress giving as much authority and support as possible to the leader on the scene, even when that individual leads a small unit.

3-19. ADP 6-0 stresses that mission command is based on mutual trust, shared understanding, and purpose. In land operations, important decisions need to made quickly and on the scene where circumstances may drastically differ from those envisioned at the start of an operation. Commanders emphasize the objective, or end state, and not the details of how to accomplish the mission. The key is that they communicate, and subordinates understand, the purpose of the operation, the intent behind the mission, key tasks, and the end state as well as all resources available. Mutual trust between commander and subordinates becomes essential. All Soldiers prepare to place the mission first, take the initiative, and act resourcefully within their commander's intent. Every commander prepares to underwrite the actions of their subordinates acting within the commander's intent and the lawful bounds placed on military actions, recognizing that land operations are the province of uncertainty and chance.

3-20. Combined arms maneuver is impossible unless commanders have the expertise and communications to synchronize Army and joint combat power. The science of control—regulating, monitoring, and directing unit actions—requires sophisticated and rugged information systems, along with a well-trained staff to employ them. Without these systems, even knowledgeable and charismatic commanders cannot control anything beyond their immediate surroundings. To an increasing degree, our ability to employ Army capabilities depends upon cyber electromagnetic activities. The degree to which we effectively protect friendly networks (wired and wireless) and exploit or degrade the enemy's has become intrinsic to combined arms.

3-21. The Army's force structure includes headquarters with specialized equipment and manned by skilled personnel at every echelon from company (commanded by a captain), to Army corps and theater armies (commanded by a lieutenant generals). These headquarters provide leadership and organization for Army forces together with any joint and multinational formations organized under them. Higher echelon Army headquarters, such as an Army corps, are often augmented with personnel from other Services and international forces to become joint or multinational task forces. In Afghanistan, Army commanders lead host-nation and international military contingents as components of the overall multinational effort.

SUPPORT JOINT AND ARMY FORCES

3-22. A significant portion of the Army's combat power is devoted to sustaining the force; not just Army units, but also other Service forces, and as required, multinational forces. Army sustainment gives our forces extraordinary endurance. That endurance permits joint forces to campaign for months and years, often in harsh environments. The joint force commander depends upon common-user logistics provided by the Army. Military expeditions throughout history have failed when disease and combat losses eroded their combat power, or a lack of supplies prevented them from seizing opportunities. However, in the 21st century, our Nation deploys large ground forces anywhere and can employ them indefinitely. U.S. Soldiers operating around the world today are the best supplied, best equipped, and healthiest American troops in history.

SUPPORT DOMESTIC CIVIL AUTHORITIES

3-23. Within the United States and its territories, the Army provides support to national, state, and local authorities. These operations fall under DSCA or state National Guard support. (The difference is administrative and does not change tactical missions.) Army units respond immediately to disasters and attacks as required by civil authorities and within limits established by law. This is one of the primary missions of the Army National Guard, which provides both DSCA and state support. The responsiveness that gives Army units their expeditionary capability is just as valuable in domestic emergencies. As required by law, the Army Corps of Engineers maintains the Nation's rivers and waterways. The corps has the primary responsibility for safeguarding communities from floods.

MOBILIZE AND INTEGRATE THE RESERVE COMPONENTS

3-24. Throughout its history, a significant portion of the Army's strength has been made up of citizen soldiers, men and women serving their country while pursuing civilian careers. Their service allows our Reserve Components—the Army National Guard and Army Reserve—to provide the Nation with a uniquely capable Army that is responsive, versatile, and tremendously powerful. Our National Guard and Reserve units provide the depth and versatility that allow us to fulfill the combatant commanders' requirements for tailored landpower.

3-25. Over the past decade, the Army quietly underwent one of the most important changes in its long history, as it transformed the Reserve Components into an integral part of the operational force. Today, Army National Guard and Army Reserve units routinely mobilize and integrate with Regular Army units within Army force packages for the combatant commanders. Guardsmen and Reservists deploy overseas tailored for both training and active operations. At home, Army National Guard units continue to support their states and territories when called out by their respective Governors. The Army National Guard fulfills homeland security and defense missions that would otherwise require Regular Army contingency forces. The depth of combat experience in the National Guard and Reserve has intangible benefits in terms of acceptance and familiarity when all three components work together in support of domestic authorities. The Reserve Components match the combatant commanders' operational requirements for landpower to the Nation's strategic needs.

JOINT INTERDEPENDENCE

3-26. American control of the global commons confers tactical, operational, and strategic advantages to Army forces. No Soldier has faced a concerted air threat in over 60 years. The Army operates helicopters without interference from enemy fighters and maneuvers forces using Air Force transports. Navy control of the sea has allowed force projection of Army units without loss for decades. Since the beginning of the space age, the United States has enjoyed unopposed access to space and critical support from American space systems.

3-27. The integration of Army forces within the joint force has never been greater. In World War II, the integration of joint capabilities occurred at the theater level with discrete missions allocated to the various Services. Friendly fire incidents involving errant naval gunfire, artillery, and close air support were not uncommon. The full effect of supporting arms usually required colossal expenditures of munitions and often killed thousands of noncombatants. Today's joint force has evolved from integration at the theater level to integration at the small-unit level. Platoon leaders can call upon air, maritime, and space-based capabilities that would have been considered science fiction by their World War II and Vietnam War counterparts.

3-28. For example, joint domination of the global commons ensures that Soldiers receive the most advanced trauma care within minutes of being wounded; their chances of survival are as high as or higher than those of a citizen severely injured in a domestic auto accident. Soldiers are statistically healthier in a combat zone than their civilian age group is at home. Consequently, the Army deploys fewer Soldiers today to theater as replacements for casualties than were deployed in the past.

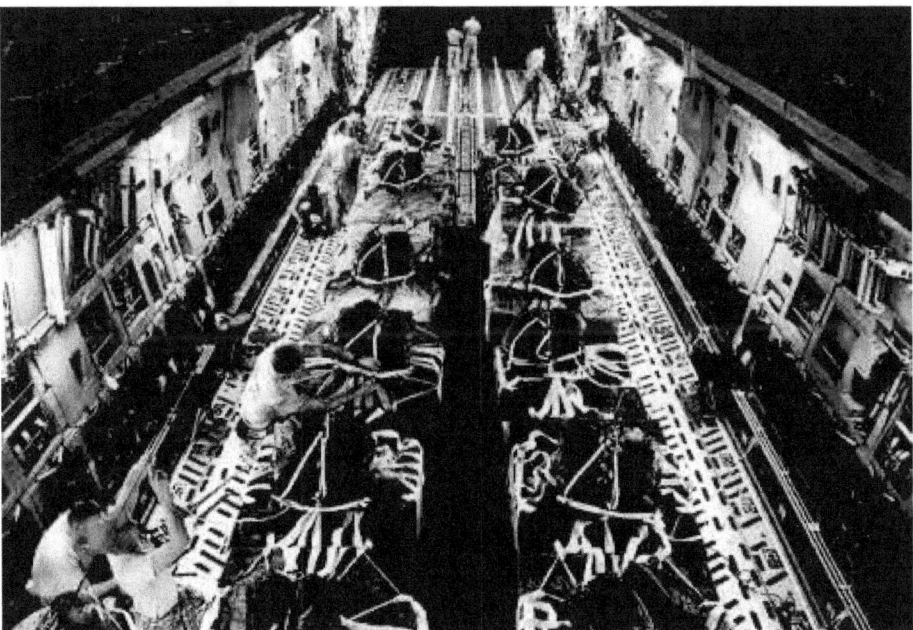

Figure 3-2. Army riggers prepare supplies for airdrop from a C-17

3-29. The tactical effects of interdependence are extraordinary and foretell new ways of operating. Small units no longer depend upon proximity to other Army units for mutual support. They are distributed widely across vast areas, dependent on an integrated joint architecture to make them unbeatable. They can employ precise and lethal firepower that uses one weapon to achieve the military effect that required tons of ordnance even a decade ago. Small units can summon lethal and nonlethal capabilities in minutes, delivered by systems potentially hundreds of miles away. Incidents of friendly fire occur but are uncommon and less frequent each year. Given the potential lethality of joint combat systems, this is not just remarkable, it is revolutionary.

This page intentionally left blank.

Chapter 4

Our Continuing Duty

To be prepared for war is one of the most effectual means of preserving peace.

President George Washington
First Annual Address to both Houses of Congress
8 January 1790

As George Washington eloquently instructed our new Nation in 1790, our peace and security depend upon our readiness to fight for it. The challenge is to prepare for a future that defies prediction even while concentrating on current operations around the globe. As the Army transitions into a leaner force, it will remain capable of rapid expansion. The Reserve Components have never been as capable as they are today, and this will continue. The all-volunteer force is our most important asset. The Army needs to lean on the experience of current leaders to develop a new generation ready to master the challenges of the future. The way the Army develops new leaders requires renewed commitment to our profession and to all who serve and have served.

WIN THE CURRENT FIGHT

4-1. Our immediate focus remains on accomplishing current missions. The commitment and performance of our Soldiers and Army Civilians continue to be extraordinary. On one hand, they continue to take the fight to our enemies; on the other hand, they take unprecedented measures to protect noncombatants. U.S. Soldiers have effectively become emissaries and coordinators within small communities. Our investment in training and leader development prepared Soldiers to persevere and overcome in this demanding environment. As we concentrate on solidifying gains made in ongoing conflicts, we will remain ready for unforeseen contingencies. The support of the American people has been, and will remain, paramount to our success. We remain mindful of their trust in us to get the mission accomplished in a way that brings credit to us and to the Nation.

Figure 4-1. Air assault in Afghanistan

DEVELOP THE FUTURE ARMY

4-2.   An unpredictable security environment requires us to develop the land force of the future as part of Joint Force 2020, while we remain flexible and ready to meet the Nation's requirements. As the Army transitions from a force shaped by counterinsurgency and stability missions, it will remain engaged in the current conflicts. The Army will prioritize its assets toward the Pacific region and Middle East and will reshape the force to support the National Military Strategy. As these defense priorities reshape the Army, we need to avoid the historic pattern of drawing down too quickly and risk losing leaders, skills, and capabilities. History demonstrates that "the war to end all wars" has never been fought. Experts continue to testify about the impact of technology and the decreasing requirement for landpower. Yet, in seeming defiance to all their predictions, "prompt and sustained combat incident to operations on land" remains decisive. We must be able to expand rapidly to meet large and unexpected contingencies—to quickly reverse the drawdown.

4-3.   The Army's ability to expand rapidly depends on four structural factors. First, the Army must maintain a strong cadre of noncommissioned and mid-grade officers to build the core of new formations when needed. Second, we will invest significantly in Army special operations forces to increase their capabilities and provide the President with more options. This endeavor will build upon the ability of our conventional and special operations units to work as a team. Third, the Army requires ready and accessible reserve forces in the Army National Guard and Army Reserve. Lastly, the Army depends upon the Nation's industrial base. The industrial base performs research and development; designs, produces, and maintains weapons systems; and provides components and parts. An effective industrial base can rapidly expand to meet a large demand. The Army cannot by itself reform or expand the industrial base. However, we can streamline and improve internal processes, allowing industrial resources of the Nation to meet Army requirements more expeditiously and efficiently. In short, the Army needs to improve its acquisition process at every level.

OPERATIONAL ADAPTABILITY

4-4. Operational adaptability is the broad measure of the Army's utility. It is based on the recognition that while we can forecast, we cannot predict the next conflict, disaster, or humanitarian crisis. Operational adaptability requires landpower that can adjust rapidly to prevent conflict, shape an operational environment, and win the Nation's wars. It requires us to operate effectively across the range of military operations while overcoming the psychological and moral challenges of land combat.

4-5. Landpower is the ubiquitous tool of the joint force—often decisive, sometimes indirect, but indispensable. Operational adaptability requires landpower that can adjust rapidly to prevent conflict, be scalable and tailorable in order to shape an operational environment, and win the Nation's wars. It continues with our strategic roles: prevent, shape, and win. Our core and enabling competencies are essential to support of the primary missions of the U.S. Armed Forces. When decisive military action occurs beyond the land domain, Soldiers remain critical for counterinsurgency, stability, and humanitarian operations for conflict prevention and termination. We continue to support the joint force with critical capabilities in space and cyberspace while fielding network infrastructure for mission command. Soldiers and Army Civilians provide intelligence collection, analysis, and synchronization. We give joint force commanders their land-based air and missile defenses for protecting key infrastructure and bases. We provide elite forces for special operations. In addition, joint force commanders rely on Army civil affairs, military police, engineers, and many other supporting capabilities.

4-6. Operational adaptability will drive changes across Army doctrine, organization, training, materiel, leadership and education, personnel, and facilities (DOTMLPF). As we enhance our operational adaptability, we have some built-in advantages. We possess highly developed skills for joint, interagency, and multinational operations. Our small-unit leadership is the best we have ever had. We have the most highly trained and best equipped individual Soldiers in our history. The Army National Guard and Army Reserve are experienced and ready, and have never been as completely integrated within the total Army. We will build on these advantages and focus on five paired characteristics, discussed below.

Depth and Versatility

4-7. The first pair of characteristics is depth and versatility. Depth is strategic—combat-ready Regular Army forces combined with an ability to mobilize, deploy, and employ our Reserve Components. Investment and regeneration of the force also contribute to strategic depth. More than a decade of war has transformed the Army

National Guard and Army Reserve into highly effective operational reserves available on a rotational basis. In addition, these forces continue to provide the President and Governors with military capabilities for the homeland, allowing the Regular Army to focus on overseas contingencies. Versatility is operational—our diverse mix of capabilities, formations, and equipment allows the Army to tailor forces to the needs of the combatant commanders. Together, depth and versatility provide options to our National leadership for scalable landpower in a complex, dynamic, and uncertain global environment.

Adaptive and Innovative

4-8. The second pair of characteristics—adaptive and innovative—centers around how we think. Although the nature of war remains constant, warfare changes constantly. American Army units have always had a reputation of swiftly mastering the challenges posed by new environments and new enemies. Our veteran leaders must continue to stress the absolute necessity of staying ahead of the enemy, of modifying procedures and drills to dominate situation, and of listening to subordinates. Leaders accept that no predetermined solutions exist; each situation requires judgment and discretion. Given the complexity inherent in land operations, leaders need to be able to adjust based on continuous assessment and accept prudent risk. Our training and leader development must emphasize and recognize creativity at every level, and we need to reward leaders for their creativity.

Flexibility and Agility

4-9. The third pair of characteristics is flexibility and agility. To achieve strategic, operational, and tactical success, we need to remain flexible and agile. Flexibility is an operational characteristic that describes our ability to conduct different joint missions across a wide range of operational environments against equally diverse threats. We remain ready for missions spanning regular and irregular warfare, humanitarian assistance, and domestic support requirements. Agility is tactical and describes the speed and effectiveness with which we transition between tactical tasks (offense, defense, stability, or DSCA) as part of decisive action. Agility depends upon mission command, collaborative planning, and decentralized execution.

Integrated and Synchronized

4-10. The fourth pair of characteristics—integrated and synchronized—addresses the conduct of operations. Army forces do not operate independently but as part of a larger, joint, interagency, and frequently multinational effort. The way we organize and operate is derived from joint interdependence. Tactically, we synchronize operations in order to maximize the effect of combined arms. We employ dissimilar capabilities in the same area and in the correct sequence to multiply our relative combat power at the decisive place and time.

Lethal and Discriminate

4-11. The last pair of characteristics sums up the Army: lethal and discriminate. The Army's mission is fighting and winning the Nation's wars. Our lethality is the basic building block that allows us to fight and win. We organize, train, and equip Soldiers to find, fix, close with, and destroy our enemies on land under a wide range of conditions. We apply our lethal power in accordance with U.S. laws and international accords. The proximity of the enemy to noncombatants and the associated risk to our Soldiers make the discriminate application of combat power one of our greatest challenges. It emphasizes our unique ability to use our weapons discretely and precisely in populated areas. Meeting this challenge requires highly professional leaders, unmatched individual expertise, and unshakeable teamwork.

SUSTAIN RESERVE COMPONENT READINESS

4-12. The Army National Guard and Army Reserve are indispensible parts of our operational Army. The Reserve Components transformed from a force held in strategic reserve for major conflicts into an operational reserve that rotates in and out of regions in support of the joint force. The Reserve Components have been essential in operations around the world including Kosovo, the Sinai, Horn of Africa, Afghanistan, and Iraq. They continue to provide essential military support to domestic authorities at the national, state, and local levels and provide humanitarian assistance and disaster relief abroad. The Reserve Components need capabilities that complement and reinforce the Regular Army through enhanced readiness including:

- Maneuver forces prepared to respond to crisis.
- Functional and multifunctional support deployed early in a crisis.
- Forces aligned to support the daily requirements of combatant commanders.

4-13. At home, the Army continues supporting civil authorities. The Army National Guard forces under their respective Governors will continue to provide most of this support. However, the ability to commit Regular Army and Army Reserve forces whenever and wherever needed gives the President an unmatched force in any domestic crisis. Largely unnoticed by the public, the Army has committed substantial planning and resources to our domestic mission, with the dual aim of improving the Army National Guard's capability and providing complementary federal military assistance in any large emergency.

Figure 4-2. An Army National Guard helicopter supports firefighters

ENHANCE THE ALL-VOLUNTEER FORCE

4-14. Throughout most of our history, the Army has been an all-volunteer force. Our combat experience since the end of the Vietnam War has only reinforced the need for a committed, all-volunteer force. Today's battlefields are demanding, training requirements are tremendous, and equipment is complex. With such high stakes, the Army can only commit operating forces to the fight made up of nothing less than experts led by professionals. The same is true of our generating force. It must be made up of professionals, military and civilian, with the experience and talent to man, train, and equip an expert operating force.

4-15. The all-volunteer force is our greatest strategic asset, providing depth, versatility, and unmatched experience to the joint force. As the Army continues to train, develop, and retain adaptive leaders, it maintains a combat-seasoned, all-volunteer force of professionals. The upcoming challenge is not just attracting and selecting the best available candidates to be Army professionals but developing them to be as good as or better than our current professionals. During the last decade of war, commanders have given young leaders unprecedented flexibility and authority to operate effectively on the battlefield. The Army will continue to build on this foundation as leaders train the force for future missions by inculcating mission command in all training. Obviously the Army needs to retain high-quality, combat experienced leaders so that they, in turn, train the next generation of Army professionals.

DEVELOP ARMY LEADERS

4-16. Combat power can be measured many ways, but the most important determinant of combat power is intangible—leadership. Leadership is the process of influencing people by providing purpose, direction, and motivation to accomplish the mission and improve the organization. Leadership multiplies all the other factors of landpower. Good leadership can overcome great disadvantages, while poor leaders can throw away major advantages in numbers and equipment.

4-17. Our Army is the premier leader development institution. We acquire the highest talent in young men and women. We test each individual continuously. We shape them through training and experience into expert practitioners. To that we add education, leader development, and most importantly, responsibility for themselves and their teammates. Outsiders are continually struck by the confidence and authority of our young men and women and astonished by what the Army asks them to perform. Responsibility comes early and for a reason. At any moment, small-unit leaders may be the difference between mission accomplishment and failure. Good leaders respond effectively to complexity and chaos, anticipate opportunities, and remain effective under stress.

4-18. Army leaders provide purpose, direction, and motivation both inside formations and beyond. Leaders demonstrate the moral and ethical compass for their organizations. They need to learn, think, and adapt as well as communicate fully, honestly, and candidly up, down, and laterally. Leaders prepare subordinates by empowering them to operate autonomously and by underwriting risk. Adaptive leaders form the nucleus of high-performing, agile teams. Mission success is realized through leaders who balance risk with the opportunity to retain the initiative.

STRENGTHEN OUR PROFESSION

4-19. During this major transition, as with previous post-war transitions, Army leaders perform as stewards of the profession. With a greater proportion of forces spending more time at home station, commanders ensure that new military expertise continues to be developed and passed down to aspiring professionals. This requires greater intellectual rigor applied to the professional military education and operational art. At the same time, Army leaders must strengthen standards and systems impacted by operational demands, such as the processes for professional certification. Army leaders ask how each course of action and decision contemplated will impact the Army profession. While the Army will find the necessary efficiencies during reductions, military effectiveness is the true hallmark of the success of our stewardship.

SOLDIERS FOR LIFE

4-20. Before he became a famous Justice of the U.S. Supreme Court, Oliver Wendell Holmes fought in many of the large battles of the Civil War. He was wounded three times. He saw friends fall in action. Two decades later, he addressed Civil War veterans on Memorial Day, May 30, 1884. He stated, "In our youth our hearts were touched with fire...." Justice Holmes expressed eloquently that for him and his comrades, military service was the single most formative period of their lives. His remarks echo the experience of today's veterans, whether career Soldiers or single-term enlistees. The overwhelming majority of today's veterans volunteered and served honorably and selflessly. Their life paths altered when they became part of the Army. The people that they became forever differed from the young people they were before donning the Army uniform. Many suffered serious wounds, endured emotional trauma, and lost close friends. Like Justice Holmes, their bonds with the Nation, its principles, and their comrades remained with them for the rest of their lives. In many ways, the veteran never leaves the Army. Time diminishes memories of separation from family, numbing fatigue, and periods of boredom. What replaces these memories is pride in awards and decorations, in shared hardship, and above all, in service to the Nation. As they pass from young men and women into middle age and beyond, their examples continue to inspire all of us.

4-21. Today less than one-half of one percent of Americans serves in the military, and only about half of them are Soldiers. Being a Soldier is far more than a job; it is a calling, a vocation. Former Chief of Staff of the Army Eric Shinseki, although badly wounded in Vietnam as a young officer, always said, "Soldiering is an affair of the heart," a phrase he adopted from General Abrams. Taking off the uniform does not mean the end of pride in one's service to the Nation. It means taking that pride, discipline, and confidence into other areas, and never forgetting that each veteran will always be part of a proud tradition of sacrifice and service.

Figure 4-3. Soldiers for life

Appendix A

Our Organization

REGULAR ARMY AND RESERVE COMPONENTS

A-1. The Army is a huge and complex organization. By law, the Army consists of Regular Army and Reserve Components under different chains of command. Functionally, the Army is made up of those forces organized for combat as part of the joint force and those organizations that support the combat units in garrison and when deployed.

A-2. Title 10, USC, establishes the basic structure of the Army made up of one Regular Army and two Reserve Components: the Regular Army, the Army Reserve, and the Army National Guard of the United States. Army Civilians support all three components.

REGULAR ARMY

A-3. The Regular Army consists of professional Soldiers supported by Army Civilians. The Regular Army is under the command of the President of the United States. Service-specific matters are the responsibility of the Secretary of the Army, exercised through the Chief of Staff of the Army. The forces of the Regular Army include units of all types necessary for prompt employment of landpower. However, in any major war or protracted conflict, the Regular Army needs units and capabilities maintained in the Army Reserve and Army National Guard.

ARMY NATIONAL GUARD

A-4. The Army National Guard has a dual role based on the Constitution. Its first role is that of a state military force. Each state, the U.S. territories, and the District of Columbia have Army National Guard units, totaling 54 state and territorial National Guards. Army National Guard forces remain under the command of their respective Governors until mobilized for Federal service. Each state or territorial Army National Guard has "The Adjutant General," a general officer appointed by the Governor who serves as its uniformed leader. As a state military force, the Governor can order the Army National Guard to state service. The Army National Guard responds to natural disasters and other domestic emergencies many times each year. While serving their states, these citizen soldiers are subject to civil laws and that state's Code of Military Justice. The Army National Guard of that state can be used for law enforcement, a task that Federal military forces cannot perform except under special circumstances. Title 32, USC, addresses the Army National Guard when serving their respective states. Like the Army Reserve, a small number of Guardsmen are on full-time active duty, in either a federal status or a state status.

Figure A-1. Army National Guard Soldiers in Afghanistan

A-5. The Army National Guard is also an operational reserve for the Regular Army. When ordered to active duty, these Soldiers become subject to the Uniform Code of Military Justice and come under the command of the combatant commanders. Army National Guard forces are organized and equipped identically with like units in the Regular Army and Army Reserve. The Department of the Army provides their equipment and much of their funding and is responsible for assessing the combat readiness of the Army National Guard. However, Title 32, USC, provides the states with latitude in recruiting, manning, and training.

ARMY RESERVE

A-6. The Army Reserve is the Army's pool of units and individuals. It is also under the command of the President, and it only serves as a federal military force. Its members are citizen soldiers mobilized when required. Most Soldiers in units serve for a period in the Regular Army and elect to continue their service in the Reserve. The Army Reserve makes up only about one-fifth of the Army's organized units, but it provides one-half of the Army's sustainment units and one-fourth of the Army's mobilization base-expansion capability. The Army Reserve is also the Army's major source of trained individual Soldiers for augmenting headquarters and filling vacancies in the Regular Army during a crisis. Many Army Reserve Soldiers are civilian professionals, such as nurses and dentists, who augment critical Army specialties. The Army Reserve provides a wide range of capabilities in response to domestic emergencies. However, the Army Reserve is not organized and manned for contingency response. A small number of Army Reservists are on full-time active duty. This status is called "Active Guard and Reserve." Army Civilians serve in Reserve centers around the country.

THE ARMY CIVILIAN CORPS

A-7. The Army has the largest civilian workforce in the Department of Defense. Army Civilians are full-time, long-service members of the profession. The Army Civilian Corps provides the complementary skills, expertise, and competence required to project, program, support, and sustain the uniformed side of the Army. Title 5, USC, governs the Army Civilian Corps.

Figure A-2. Army Civilian Corps members

A-8. Army Civilians have assumed increased levels of responsibility and greater authority since the Army transitioned from a conscript to a professional volunteer force. Army Civilians serve in 540 occupational fields spanning 31 career programs. Over 23,000 Army Civilians deployed to Afghanistan and Iraq in support of the uniformed Services since 2001. They held senior leadership and mission critical positions in operating forces and key positions in the generating force. Army Civilians are committed to serving the Nation. They take the same oath as Army officers and members of Congress, solemnly swearing that they will support and defend the Constitution. Like their uniformed counterparts, Army Civilians are expected to live the Army Values and prepare for unforeseen future threats.

CONTRACTORS

A-9. Contractors are not members of the Army profession; however, they provide valuable support and augmentation to the capabilities of the Profession of Arms and the Army Civilian Corps, both stateside and overseas. Hired under contractual terms for specific tasks of a specified duration, they provide essential skills and perform technical and administrative tasks that allow Army professionals to focus on their primary missions. Contractors are an important part of any current or future Army effort.

FUNCTIONAL STRUCTURE

A-10. Functionally, the Army divides into operating forces and the generating force. In broad terms, operating forces deploy and fight while the generating force gets them ready.

OPERATING FORCES

A-11. Operating forces consist of units organized, trained, and equipped to deploy and fight. They include about two-thirds of the Regular Army, and three-fourths of the Army's total force. The Secretary of Defense assigns these units to the various combatant commanders. Operating forces are modular. They consist of interchangeable units grouped under various headquarters. When a combatant commander specifies the capabilities needed, the Army provides tailored force packages to provide those capabilities. In addition to general purpose forces, the Army also provides the largest element of the joint special operations forces. Army special operations forces include several special forces groups, the Ranger Regiment, civil affairs units, military information support units, and special operations aviation.

THE GENERATING FORCE

A-12. The generating force mans, trains, equips, deploys, and ensures the readiness of all Army forces. The generating force consists of Army organizations whose primary mission is to generate and sustain the operating forces of the Army. It consists of those organizations identified in Army Regulation 10-87 not assigned to a combatant commander under the "Forces for Unified Commands Memorandum." Therefore the generating force remains under the command of the Department of the Army. The training base provides military skills and a professional education to every Soldier—as well as to members of the other Services and multinational partners. The generating force is also the Army's principal interface with the commercial sector. Our Nation's industrial base provides equipment and sustainment for the Army, which is managed by the various headquarters of the generating force. Army installations are power projection platforms required to train forces and serve as departure points. Once operating forces deploy, the generating force provides the sustainment that Soldiers need for their missions, as well as specified support provided by the Army to the other Services. The generating force focuses on departmental (Title 10, USC) tasks including—

- Recruiting.
- Maintaining.

- Organizing.
- Servicing.
- Supplying.
- Training.
- Mobilizing.
- Demobilizing.
- Administering (including the morale and welfare of personnel).
- Constructing, outfitting, and repairing military equipment.
- Equipping (including research and development).
- Constructing, maintaining, and repairing buildings, structures, and utilities as well as acquiring real property.

This page intentionally left blank.

Appendix B

The Battles and Campaigns of the Army

ARMY FLAG

B-1. The Army's history is reflected in the battle and campaign streamers that adorn the Army flag. The Army flag honors all who served and are serving, reminding each American that our place today as the world's preeminent landpower was not achieved quickly or easily but built on the sacrifices from the Revolution through today. Additional information about these campaigns is available on line at http://www.army.mil/info/history/.

Figure B-1. The Army flag with streamers

EARLY AMERICAN HISTORY: 1775 -1916

B-2. From its establishment in 1775 until the end of the 19th century, Army forces fought only on the North American Continent. Only in the last decade of the 19th century did we deploy forces to distant conflicts. In size, the Army varied from a token force left after the Revolution to the large armies of the Civil War. For most of this period, a small force of regulars served on the frontiers, and the states supplied militia and volunteer units in times of emergency.

REVOLUTIONARY WAR

B-3. Following the initial engagements in Massachusetts, the Second Continental Congress established "the American Continental Army" on 14 June 1775. Eight more years of war followed. During the Revolutionary War, the Army earned 15 streamers listed in table B-1.

Table B-1. Revolutionary War streamers

• Boston	• Guilford Court House	• Saratoga
• Brandywine	• Long Island	• Savannah
• Charleston	• Monmouth	• Ticonderoga
• Cowpens	• Princeton	• Trenton
• Germantown	• Quebec	• Yorktown

WAR OF 1812

B-4. The Army expanded to fight the British in the War of 1812. Soldiers like Winfield Scott trained Army units capable of standing up to the British on the Northern Frontier. Andrew Jackson used regulars and militia at New Orleans to crush the largest British army sent to North America. That victory, coupled with naval successes, established our ability to defend U.S. territory against the European powers. During the War of 1812, the Army earned 6 streamers listed in table B-2.

Table B-2. War of 1812 streamers

• Bladensburg	• Chippewa	• McHenry
• Canada	• Lundy's Lane	• New Orleans

MEXICAN WAR

B-5. In 1846, the Army fought Mexico and extended the Nation's borders to the Pacific Ocean. The war again demonstrated the need for the Regular Army to fight alongside militia forces. During the Mexican War, the Army earned 10 streamers listed in table B-3.

Table B-3. Mexican War streamers

• Buena Vista	• Contreras	• Palo Alto
• Cerro Gordo	• Molino del Rey	• Resaca de la Palma
• Chapultepec	• Monterey	• Vera Cruz
• Churubusco		

CIVIL WAR

B-6. In 1861, the Civil War tore the Nation apart. The Army grew dramatically—in size, capability, and technological sophistication—during four years of war. Forced to fight war on a continental scale against superbly led opponents, Union forces developed skills in tactics, operational art, logistics, and inter-Service cooperation that rivaled and sometimes exceeded the great European powers. During the Civil War, the Army earned 25 streamers listed in table B-4.

Table B-4. Civil War streamers

• Antietam	• Fredericksburg	• Petersburg
• Appomattox	• Gettysburg	• Shenandoah
• Atlanta	• Henry and Donelson	• Shiloh
• Bull Run	• Manassas	• Spotsylvania
• Chancellorsville	• Mississippi River	• Sumter
• Chattanooga	• Murfreesborough	• Valley
• Chickamauga	• Nashville	• Vicksburg
• Cold Harbor	• Peninsula	• Wilderness
• Franklin		

INDIAN WARS

B-7. The Army fought against Native Americans until the beginning of the 20th century. In these bitter conflicts, the Army fought the finest individual warriors it ever faced. It fought with all-volunteer forces, including all-black cavalry and infantry regiments. Serving under the flag of the United States, Native American scouts became vital members of Army units as the wars moved onto the Great Plains. During the Indian Wars, the Army earned 14 streamers listed in table B-5.

Table B-5. Indian Wars streamers

• Apaches	• Creeks	• Pine Ridge
• Bannocks	• Little Big Horn	• Seminoles
• Black Hawk	• Miami	• Tippecanoe
• Cheyennes	• Modocs	• Utes
• Comanches	• Nez Perces	

WAR WITH SPAIN

B-8. The Spanish-American War of 1898 exposed serious deficiencies with the Army. Mobilization, deployment, and sustainment were a debacle, but fortunately Spain lacked the resources to counter. After defeating Spanish forces in Cuba and the Philippines, the Army accepted new responsibilities as a global expeditionary force and initiated major reforms to improve combat readiness. During the War with Spain, the Army earned 3 streamers:

- Manila.
- Puerto Rico.
- Santiago.

CHINA RELIEF EXPEDITION

B-9. Now almost forgotten, Soldiers fought in China during the long period of strife at the beginning of the 20th century. During the China Relief Expedition, the Army earned 3 streamers:

- Peking.
- Tientsin.
- Yang-Tsun.

PHILIPPINE INSURRECTION

B-10. After seizing the Philippines from Spain, Soldiers fought a bloody counterinsurgency in the jungles of that archipelago. During the Philippine Insurrection, the Army earned 11 streamers listed in table B-6.

Table B-6. Philippine Insurrection streamers

• Cavite	• Malolos	• San Isidro
• Iloilo	• Manila	• Tarlac
• Jolo	• Mindanao	• Zapote
• Laguna de Bay	• San Fabian	

MEXICAN EXPEDITION

B-11. When internal conflict in Mexico spread across the border into the United States, U.S. units deployed on the border and moved into northern Mexico, clashing with Mexican troops and irregular forces. During the Mexican Expedition, the Army earned the "Mexico" streamer.

MODERN AMERICAN HISTORY: 1917—PRESENT

B-12. World War I forced the United States to create an Army that could fight the most powerful and professional force in Europe. It also initiated awareness within the Army that our constabulary wars were over, and we had become a great power.

WORLD WAR I

B-13. The war forced our small, lightly equipped Army to expand to unprecedented size. Millions of Americans volunteered or were drafted to create the American Expeditionary Forces (AEF). By 1918, the AEF became a force capable of defeating the German army. During World War I, the Army earned 13 streamers listed in table B-7.

Table B-7. World War I streamers

• Aisne	• Meuse-Argonne	• Somme Offensive
• Aisne-Marne	• Montdidier-Noyon	• St. Mihiel
• Cambrai	• Oise-Aisne	• Vittoria Veneto
• Champagne-Marne	• Somme Defensive	• Ypres-Lys
• Lys		

WORLD WAR II

B-14. Nazi Germany, Fascist Italy, and Imperial Japan forced the Army to recognize that U.S. security was inseparable from global security. We fielded the largest Army in American history and fought simultaneously in North America, Asia, the Pacific, the Mediterranean, and Northern Europe. Soldiers not only fought the Axis Powers; they rebuilt the once-defeated armies of France, China, and other allied forces. By the end of the war, the Army's 89 divisions were the best equipped, best supplied, and most mobile land forces in the world. During World War II, the Army earned 38 streamers listed in table B-8.

Table B-8. World War II streamers

• Air Offensive, Europe	• China Defensive	• Northern Solomons
• Air Offensive, Japan	• China Offensive	• Papua
• Aleutian Islands	• East Indies	• Philippine Islands
• Algeria–French Morocco	• Eastern Mandates	• Po Valley
• Antisubmarine	• Egypt–Libya	• Rhineland
• Anzio	• Guadalcanal	• Rome-Arno
• Ardennes-Alsace	• India-Burma	• Ryukyus
• Bismarck Archipelago	• Leyte	• Sicily
• Burma	• Luzon	• Southern France
• Central Burma	• New Guinea	• Southern Philippines
• Central Europe	• Normandy	• Tunisia
• Central Pacific	• Northern Apennines	• Western Pacific
• Naples-Foggia, Air and Ground	• Northern France	

KOREAN WAR AND VIETNAM WAR

B-15. The conflicts in Korea and Vietnam were limited in terms of objectives from fear of another global war, this time with nuclear weapons. Even the nomenclature of war and the formality of declaring it changed. Both Asian wars forced the United States to deploy large conventional forces and maintain the draft for nearly a quarter century.

Korea

B-16. During the Korean War, the Army earned 10 streamers listed in table B-9.

Table B-9. Korean War streamers

• CCF Intervention	• UN Offensive	• UN Defensive
• First UN Counteroffensive	• CCF Spring Offensive	• Third Korean Winter
• UN Summer-Fall Offensive	• Second Korean Winter	• Korea, Summer 1953
• Korea, Summer-Fall 1952		
CCF Communist Chinese Forces	UN United Nations	

Vietnam

B-17. During the Vietnam War, the Army earned 17 streamers listed in table B-10.

Table B-10. Vietnam War streamers

• Tet Counteroffensive	• Counteroffensive, Phase III	• Consolidation I
• Counteroffensive, Phase II	• Counteroffensive, Phase V	• Consolidation II
• Counteroffensive, Phase IV	• Counteroffensive, Phase VI	• Defense
• Tet 69 Counteroffensive	• Summer-Fall 1969	• Cease Fire
• Sanctuary Counteroffensive	• Advisory	• Winter-Spring 1970
• Counteroffensive, Phase VII	• Counteroffensive	

ARMED FORCES EXPEDITIONS

B-18. Other post-war conflicts included military occupation of the Dominican Republic in 1965, combat operations in Grenada in 1983, and forcible removal of Dictator Manuel Noriega in Panama in 1989. During these Armed Forces expeditions, the Army earned 3 streamers:

- Dominican Republic.
- Grenada.
- Panama.

SOUTHWEST ASIA

B-19. A crisis in 1990 erupted after Saddam Hussein's seizure of Kuwait. The Army quickly mobilized and deployed 500,000 Soldiers equipped with the most advanced equipment. Hussein's forces were crushed in one of the most lopsided wars in history. During actions in southwest Asia, the Army earned 3 streamers:

- Cease-Fire.
- Defense of Saudi Arabia.
- Liberation and Defense of Kuwait.

KOSOVO

B-20. Ethnic cleansing in the former Yugoslavia led to the commitment of Army forces in a peace enforcement operation in the province of Kosovo. During operations in Kosovo, the Army earned 2 streamers:

- Kosovo Air Campaign.
- Kosovo Defense Campaign.

WAR ON TERRORISM

B-21. In the aftermath of the attacks of September 2001, Army forces deployed to Afghanistan and Iraq. American-led forces drove Saddam Hussein and the Taliban from power in fast moving campaigns notable for the relatively small numbers of troops and the sophistication of joint operations. American forces, alongside multinational and Iraqi forces, stabilized Iraq to conclude Operations Iraqi Freedom and New Dawn successfully. In Afghanistan, U.S. forces toppled the brutal Taliban regime and denied sanctuary to Al Qaeda and its surrogates. During the War on Terrorism, the Army earned 8 streamers listed in table B-11.

Table B-11. War on Terrorism streamers

• Consolidation I	• Iraqi Surge	• National Resolution
• Global War on Terrorism	• Liberation of Afghanistan	• Transition of Iraq
• Iraqi Governance	• Liberation of Iraq	

This page intentionally left blank.

Source Notes

This section lists sources by page number. Where material appears in a paragraph, it lists both the page number and paragraph number.

Front cover   Photos. Available at
http://www.flickr.com/photos/soldiersmediacenter/6966661875,
http://www.flickr.com/photos/soldiersmediacenter/7375267670, and
http://www.flickr.com/photos/soldiersmediacenter/3993449914.

Inside cover   Photo of door gunner. Available at www.defenseimagery.mil.

"I am an American Soldier.": *Soldier's Creed*. Available at
http://www.army.mil/values/soldiers.html.

Inside page   Photo of Army Civilian. Available at www.defenseimagery.mil.

"I am an Army Civilian—": *Army Civilian Creed*. Available at
http://www.army.mil/values/corps.html.

v   introductory figure. Two Soldiers in the snow. Available at
http://www.flickr.com/photos/soldiersmediacenter/6915949719.

vi   "I, _____, do solemnly swear ...":. Available at
http://www.army.mil/values/oath.html.

1-1   "[T]he United States Army remains ...": *2012 Army Posture Statement: The Nation's Force of Decisive Action* (Washington DC: Government Printing Office, 2012), 2.

1-3   fig. 1-1. Photo of Soldier and crowd. Available at
http://www.flickr.com/photos/soldiersmediacenter/7195227238.

1-4   fig. 1-2. Photo of medic and child. Available at www.defenseimagery.mil.

1-5   "The Army is globally engaged...": General Raymond T. Odierno, *The Army Vision* (2012). Available at http://armylive.dodlive.mil/index.php/2012/05/army-vision/.

1-6   fig. 1-3. Photo of multinational training. Available at www.defenseimagery.mil.

1-7   "(a) It is the intent of Congress...": Title 10, United States Code, Section 3062. Available at http://uscode.house.gov/uscode-cgi/.

1-8   "The mission of the ...": Mission of the United States Army. Available at
http://www.army.mil/info/organization/.

2-1   "[We will] foster continued commitment...": *Marching Orders: 38th Chief of Staff, U.S. Army* (2012), 2. Available at
http://usarmy.vo.llnwd.net/e2/c/downloads/234187.pdf.

2-1   fig. 2-1. Photo of medical evacuation. Available at
http://www.flickr.com/photos/soldiersmediacenter/5857537134.

2-2   2-1. "assured reliance on the character ...": *Merriam-Webster's Collegiate Dictionary, tenth edition* (Springfield, Massachusetts: Merriam-Webster, Incorporated, 1995), 1269.

2-3   fig. 2-2. Photo of Soldier. Available at http://www.flickr.com/photos/soldiersmediacenter/5418579692/.

2-6   fig. 2-3. Photo of tank. Available at http://www.flickr.com/photos/soldiersmediacenter/5392511279.

2-6   2-18. "shall be bound by...": "Article VI," *Constitution of the United States.* Available at http://www.archives.gov/exhibits/charters/constitution_transcript.htm.

2-7   2-19. "While we are guarding...": General Raymond T. Odierno citing General Creighton Adams, "Foreword: The Profession of Arms," *Military Review: The Professional Journal of the U.S. Army* (September 2011), 3.

2-8   fig. 2-4. Photo of Old Guard. Available at www.defenseimagery.mil.

2-9   2-25. "...and that I will well and...": *Oath of Commissioned Officers.* Available at http://www.army.mil/values/officers.html.

3-1   "The synergy that results...": Joint Publication 1, *Doctrine for the Armed Forces of the United States,* (Washington DC: Government Printing Office, 2007), I-2.

3-2   3-2. "In all the mission areas...": *2012 Army Strategic Planning Guidance* (Washington DC: Government Printing Office, 2012), 16.

3-6   fig. 3-1. Photo of armor. Available at www.defenseimagery.mil.

3-9   fig. 3-2. Photo of Army riggers. Available at www.defenseimagery.mil.

4-1   "To be prepared for war...": President George Washington in first annual address to Congress. Available at http://teachingamericanhistory.org/. TeachingAmericanHistory.org is a project of the Ashbrook Center at Ashland University.

4-2   fig. 4-1. Photo of Chinook. Available at http://www.flickr.com/photos/soldiersmediacenter/6872916011.

4-6   fig. 4-2. Photo of firefighting. Available at www.defenseimagery.mil.

4-7   4-20. "In our youth our hearts...": Richard A. Posner, ed., *The Essential Holmes: Selections From the Letters, Speeches, Judicial Opinions, and Other Writings of Oliver Wendell Holmes, Jr.* (Chicago: University of Chicago Press, 1992), 80-87.

4-8   4-21. "Soldiering is an affair...": of General Creighton Abrams, as quoted in General Shinseki's retirement address. General Eric K. Shinseki, "Farewell Speech," Retirement Ceremony, Fort Myer, Virginia, 11 June 2003.

4-8   fig. 4-3. Photo of veteran. Available at www.defenseimagery.mil.

A-2   fig. A-1. Photo of ARNG troops. Available at www.defenseimagery.mil.

A-3   fig. A-2. Photo of Army Civilians. Available at www.defenseimagery.mil.

B-1   fig. B-1. Photo of Army flag. Available at http://usarmy.vo.llnwd.net/e2/rv5_downloads/symbols/ColorsHigh.jpg.

Back cover   Photo of Soldier. Available at www.defenseimagery.mil.

Glossary

The glossary lists acronyms.

ADP	Army doctrine publication
ADRP	Army doctrine reference publication
AEF	American Expeditionary Forces
ARNG	Army National Guard
DA	Department of the Army
DODD	Department of Defense directive
DOTMLPF	doctrine, organization, training, materiel, leadership and education, personnel, and facilities
DSCA	defense support of civil authorities
GI	government issue (slang for Soldier)
JP	joint publication
U.S.	United States
USC	United States Code

This page intentionally left blank.

References

Field manuals and selected joint publications are listed by new number followed by old number.

REQUIRED PUBLICATIONS

This document must be available to intended users of this publication.

JP 1-02. *Department of Defense Dictionary of Military and Associated Terms.* 8 November 2010.

RELATED PUBLICATIONS

These documents contain relevant supplemental information.

JOINT PUBLICATIONS

Most joint publications are available online:
> http://www.dtic.mil/doctrine/new_pubs/jointpub.htm.

JP 1. *Doctrine for the Armed Forces of the United States.* 2 May 2007.

JP 3-0. *Joint Operations.* 11 August 2011.

ARMY PUBLICATIONS

Most Army doctrinal publications are available online: http://www.apd.army.mil/.

ADP 3-0. *Unified Land Operations.* 10 October 2011.

ADP 6-0. *Mission Command.* 17 May 2012.

ADRP 3-0. *Unified Land Operations.* 16 May 2012.

ADRP 6-22. *Army Leadership.* 1 August 2012.

Army Regulation 10-87. *Army Commands, Army Service Component Commands, and Direct Reporting Units.* 4 September 2007.

Field Manual 27-10. *The Law of Land Warfare.* 18 July 1956.

OTHER PUBLICATIONS

"Forces for Unified Commands Memorandum."

2012 Army Posture Statement. Washington, DC: Office of the Chief of Staff, Army. 2012. Available at https://secureweb2.hqda.pentagon.mil/VDAS_ArmyPostureStatement/2012/APS2012.pdf.

AJP-01. *Allied Joint Doctrine.* Available at https://nsa.nato.int/protected/unclass/ap/AJP-01(D).pdf.

Army Civilian Creed. Available at http://www.army.mil/values/corps.html.

Army Mission. Available at http://www.army.mil/info/organization/.

Army Strategic Planning Guidance. 2012. Available at
http://usarmy.vo.llnwd.net/e2/c/downloads/243816.pdf.

Defense Strategic Guidance.
http://www.defense.gov/news/Defense_Strategic_Guidance.pdf

Department of Defense Directive 5100.01. *Functions of the Department of Defense and Its Major Components.* 21 December 2010.

Marching Orders: 38th Chief of Staff, U.S. Army: America's Force of Decisive Action (2012), 2. Available at
http://usarmy.vo.llnwd.net/e2/c/downloads/234187.pdf.

Merriam-Webster's Collegiate Dictionary, tenth edition. Springfield, Massachusetts: Merriam-Webster, Incorporated, 1995.

National Defense Strategy of the United States of America. Washington, DC: U.S. Government Printing Office, 2008.

National Military Strategy of the United States of America. Washington, DC: U.S. Government Printing Office, 2011.

National Security Strategy of the United States of America. Washington, DC: U.S. Government Printing Office, 2010.

Oath of Commissioned Officers. Available at
http://www.army.mil/values/officers.html.

Odierno, Raymond T. "Foreword: The Profession of Arms." *Military Review: The Professional Journal of the U.S. Army* (September 2011): 2–4.

Posner, Richard A., ed. *The Essential Holmes: Selections From the Letters, Speeches, Judicial Opinions, and Other Writings of Oliver Wendell Holmes, Jr.* Chicago: University of Chicago Press, 1992.

Shinseki, Eric K. "Farewell Speech." Retirement Ceremony. Fort Myer, Virginia: 11 June 2003.

Soldier's Creed. Available at http://www.army.mil/values/soldiers.html.

The Army Profession: 2012, After More than a Decade of Conflict. Blackwell, OK: Schatz Publishing Group, 2012.

The Army Vision. Available at
http://armylive.dodlive.mil/index.php/2012/05/army-vision/.

The Constitution of the United States.

Title 5, United States Code. Government Organization and Employees.

Title 10, United States Code. Armed Forces.

Title 32, United States Code. National Guard.

WEB SITES

Army history. Available at http://www.army.mil/info/history/.

Army photos. Available at http://www.flickr.com/photos/soldiersmediacenter/ and www.defenseimagery.mil.

United States Code. Available at http://uscode.house.gov/.

RECOMMENDED READING

Army 2020: Generating Health and Discipline in the Force Ahead of the Strategic Reset. Washington, DC: Headquarters, Department of the Army, 2012. Available at http://usarmy.vo.llnwd.net/e2/c/downloads/235822.pdf.

Stewart, Richard W., ed. *American Military History. Vol. I, The United States Army and the Forging of a Nation, 1775-1917.* Washington, DC: Center of Military History, United States Army, 2010. Available at http://www.history.army.mil/books/AMH-V1/index.htm.

Stewart, Richard W., ed. *American Military History. Vol. 2, The U.S. Army in a Global Era, 1917-2003.* Washington, DC: Center of Military History, United States Army, 2010. Available at http://www.history.army.mil/books/AMH-V2/index.htm.

Wilson, John B. *U.S. Army Campaign Streamers: Colors of Courage Since 1775.* Arlington, Virginia: Institute of Land Warfare, The Association of the United States Army, 2009. Available at http://www.ausa.org/publications/ilw/ilw_pubs/specialreports/Documents/CampaignStreamers.pdf.

Wright, Donald P., ed. *Vanguard of Valor: Small Unit Actions in Afghanistan.* Fort Leavenworth, Kansas: Combat Studies Institute Press, US Army Combined Arms Center, 2011. Available at http://usacac.army.mil/cac2/cgsc/carl/download/csipubs/VanguardOfValor.pdf.

REFERENCED FORMS

DA Form 2028. *Recommended Changes to Publications and Blank Forms.*

This page intentionally left blank.

By Order of the Secretary of the Army:

RAYMOND T. ODIERNO
General, United States Army
Chief of Staff

Official:

JOYCE E. MORROW
Administrative Assistant to the
Secretary of the Army
1225701

DISTRIBUTION:

Active Army, Army National Guard, and United States Army Reserve: To be distributed in accordance with the initial distribution number (IDN) 110510, requirements for ADP 1.

**THE UNITED STATES ARMY—
THE STRENGTH OF THE NATION**

PIN: 103140-000

www.ingramcontent.com/pod-product-compliance
Lightning Source LLC
Chambersburg PA
CBHW082327290526
45793CB00009B/908